richard paul hinkle

good
wine
the new basics

Table of Contents

introduction

It's Just "Grape Juice"

The goal of this book is to show you that wine is an easy beverage to get to know and that the many people who profit by promoting arrogance and pretension in wine are wrong. Wine is just grape juice. It's pretty good grape juice, sure, and if it's handled well—grapes grown in certain locations have more character—it can even be special grape juice, grape juice with an attitude, with an identity, with a personality. But it's still just grape juice that's been fermented and, perhaps, aged a bit.

Remember that when someone's trying to sell you a bill of goods: grape juice. It's easy to pop the bubble of hoity and toity as someone's expounding, on and on *ad infinitum*, by saying to yourself, "grape juice."

The best means I have found to make wine friendlier is to demonstrate that your palate belongs to you, and need not be influenced unduly by any wine expert, including me. Not that you can't draw from the experience of others, but when the grape juice hits the palate you get to decide: Like it; don't like it; drink it if someone else pays for it. That's the main menu, those are the main choices. It's as simple as that, and if I can convince you of that you'll never be intimidated by a wine, or by a wine maven, again.

Think of it as going to a symphony performance. You can enjoy a symphony without knowing the difference between a French horn and an English horn (or the fact that one is not French and the other is not a horn). But you can also gain a greater understanding of the music if you *choose* to delve beyond the basics. That's the fun of learning. If you so choose. Even so, keep close to the bottom line: It's just grape juice.

Your Palate:
Where We Start

The very touchstone of this book is that you get to choose what you like and what you don't like when it comes to wine. Just as it is with art and automobiles, literature and music, it can be most instructive to delve into the subject more than toe-deep. Not only is it satisfying to expand your horizons with new information, but it gives you the opportunity to justify—to yourself, if to no one else—your choices, your selections. While it's perfectly fine to say that "I prefer this Zinfandel to that Rhône," you can go forward far more confidently when you can say "I like the lively spiciness of the Zinfandel a bit more than I like the dustiness and warmth of the Rhône."

I have always wondered why it is that someone who would never let another dictate his or her taste in music or art turns around and begs, "What kind of wine should I drink?" My short answer is, "Try 10, you'll like three, you can afford two—those are the ones!"

My long answer is this book, which will attempt to draw you into the vast enjoyment that is available to you when you gleefully expose your tastes to the wondrous variety that is wine today. Not only do the usual suspects—France and California—continue to make exciting wines, but it is perfectly exhilarating to taste equally enchanting offerings from Italy, Spain, Germany, Portugal, Australia, Chile, New Zealand, South Africa, Argentina, and other places too numerous to mention. Heck, even here in the U.S., we've gone so far beyond the Golden State, from the "knowns" of Washington and New York, to the up-and-comers of Oregon, Ohio, Texas, Minnesota, Missouri, Arkansas, and many others. What fun!

Why Wine?
Or, It's Just a Bunch of Grapes Got Caught in a Squeeze!

You're going to run into a lot of folk who get off (or make their living) trying to convince you that wine is difficult. It's only difficult if you let it be. Wine is nothing more than fermented grape juice, a bunch of grapes that got caught in a squeeze.

The greatest thing about wine is that it is a social beverage. Wine brings people together. Family. Friends, old and new. Bring wine to the dinner table and it improves the taste of the food you eat and the conversations you engage in. It even improves your digestion. Imagine that.

The most civilizing of beverages, wine has long been a part of religious ceremony, from the "Miracle of Cana" onward. Some of us taste wine as the consecrated blood of Christ, others of us find other, lasting spiritual values in this miraculous juice. (The Dalai Lama teaches that happiness is the primary goal of life, and good wine certainly furthers that end.)

Most interesting is the fact that what we have intuited, over the ages, as natural health benefits, are now being proven by rigorous studies. We are certain now that moderate consumption of wine—a glass or two a day—reduces heart and circulatory risk by up to 50 percent over those who either drink too much…or none at all. Think about that. It is better to drink a little than not to imbibe at all. (Unless, of course, your body cannot properly metabolize alcohol. Perhaps 10 percent of adults are susceptible to alcohol, and should not consume it in any form, at any time.) Alcohol, like any other drug, has a beneficial dosage and a toxic dosage, and that varies from person to person. For some, any is too much.

The bottom line is this: Wine brings people together. In a crazy and often disjointed world, that is rather a blessing, don't you think?

wines

The Six Wine "Types":
You Can Make 'em All from Zinfandel Grapes

This is my favorite exercise from all the wine appreciation classes I've ever taught, demonstrating—and tasting—how you can make each of the six basic wine types…using just one grape variety. It is, simply enough, the most dramatic means of showing how wine is made. And, as you taste the full range of the wines—knowing that their production came through the varied manipulation of the same grape variety—you have a startlingly clear understanding, I think, of how it all works and how logical the totality of it is.

We're going to use Zinfandel in this exercise because it is the most versatile grape variety extant (though, if you're like me, you'll think Pinot Noir in the back of your mind because of its greater subtlety in all its wine forms). Let's make our white wine first. The trick to making white wine is to separate the juice from the skins as soon as possible—almost immediately—so that the wine extracts none of the skin's pigment. What you need to know for this exercise is that the juice of nearly all wine grape varieties is innately clear, so we're going to end up with a white wine if we ferment only the juice. Remember, with wine grapes, color is only skin deep.

Want a rosé? Easy enough. This time we'll ferment the juice in contact with the pigment-rich skins for just a short time, since we want only a "blush" of color. The more color we want, the longer time we leave the juice on the skins. There is a whole continuum of color, you see, from near clear to near-black red. For both white and rosé wines, we can either let the fermentation run its full course to end up with a "dry" wine (one absent fermentable sugars), or stop the fermentation to retain a fruit-enhancing amount of residual sugar.

To produce a red wine? Just allow the fermentation to run its full course in contact with the skins—usually about a week—and we'll have a lusty, bold, dry red wine.

Be it cheese or wine, fermentation is one of nature's miracles. This is how simple it all is: If you were to crush a handful of ripe wine grapes in your hands—and stand there patiently for a week—the grape-skin-borne yeast would convert the sugar-rich juice (wine grapes are about one-fourth sugar) into ethanol and carbon dioxide. Naturally. The carbon dioxide would dissipate into the air, and you would have alcohol-preserved grape juice. Wine.

For your basic sparkling wine, we're going to do an ordinary white wine fermentation with fruit that's slightly under-ripe—we want all the crisp acidity we can get in the finished product—then we're going to add sugar and ferment the wine a second time. Only this time, we're not going to allow that carbon dioxide to bubble off into thin air. We're going to keep it in the form of pressurized bubbles, the essence of champagne and other great sparklers from around the world.

For a dessert wine, like Port, we would stop the fermentation prior to dryness by adding a neutral brandy (fortified wine, by the way).

Aperitif wines are, curiously, handled similarly to dessert wines, except that the fermentation is usually stopped early (to create a dry wine) and an herbal infusion is added to create a unique flavor profile.

So, now you know how wine is made. Pretty easy, eh? (The sections that follow are in order of use, rather than in order of production technique.)

Aperitif Wines:

A Little Something to Amuse the Mouth

The French have a phrase for those light sorbets that are used to "cleanse the palate" between courses of formal meals: *amuse bouche* ("amuse the mouth"). That's what aperitif wines are, really, a little something to prime the pump of your palate, to get your mouth and your digestive system watering for the meal that is to follow. A little something to amuse your mouth.

My favorite aperitif wines are the dry Sherries, particularly the Spanish *finos*, wines so delicate, so ethereal that they act like Siren temptresses, taunting your taste buds with wild promises of fulfillment. *Finos* have less alcohol than the fuller, sweeter Sherries, and are artfully structured to leave you wanting more (mainly, the meal that you expect to follow).

Many sparkling wines work perfectly as appetizer wines, particularly the dry bubblies, usually labeled *brut* or *savage*. (Curiously, sparkling wines labeled sec, which means "dry," are markedly sweeter than those labeled *brut*.)

Dry white wines also work well before the entrée course. Dry German wines with the Kabinett designation will tempt your tongue, as will a dry Sauvignon or Fumé Blanc or a dry Alsatian white.

There are also the dry vermouths, wines that have been "infused" with dried herbs, to consider. Some people, particularly those who have traveled in France, lean toward white wine spritzers—a dry white wine mixed with sparkling water— or the artful blend of sparkling wine and cassis (blackcurrant liqueur) known as *kir* (named for a WWII Burgundian resistance movement hero).

Try each of the above. Experiment. You may find some repulsive, some mediocre, and a few absolutely enchanting. Those are the ones to stick with. Which, of course, is what this whole wine exercise is about: Finding and defining your own palate.

White Wines:
Oh, What a Wonderful World

To characterize white wines as "feminine" actually serves to expand the range of styles, weights, and flavors available. Indeed, the array may even exceed that of red wines.

As you know, white wines are made by fermenting only the juice of the grape. After that, all bets are off. The wine can be made bone-dry. It can be made with just a hint of residual sugar (oft called "off-dry"). It can be made cloyingly sweet, with sugar coming out its ears.

If you start with Sauvignon Blanc, you can let the fruit ripen fully, where fresh grass and honeydew melon leap out at you (*a la Sancerre*), or you can pick it earlier and aim for a steely, mineral-laden Graves style. If you allow the *botrytis* mold to get involved, you aim for the honey-rich Sauternes goal of providing dessert perfection.

Chardonnay is the most malleable of wines, the winemaker's toy. Go lean and crisp like Chablis, or go for full-throttle-ripe and tons of oak like the late and unlamented "California style." There is plenty of room between the two for a winemaker to put a purely personal stamp on a wine.

Then there are grapes that go their own way. White Riesling shows off fruit purity of apricot and grapefruit that rings clear be it from the Rhine or Mosel, New York, or New Zealand. The Gewürz in Gewürztraminer means "spicy," and nutmeg and cinnamon spice it is, from Alsace to Anderson Valley. Both of these are wonderfully suited to the influence of *botrytis* for dessert beauties that can stand alone or complement an equal array of sweets.

Please don't forget the "little" whites. The floral-scented Chenin Blanc, the silky Pinot Blanc, the crisp, steeliness of Pinot Grigio/Pinot Gris, the aromatic glory of Muscats Blanc, Canelli, and Alexandria. They expand the category with style and flair.

Rosé Wines:
Not Just Another Pretty Face

For the longest time, Americans passed off rosé wines as little more than sweet pink leftovers, some of which (Lancer's and Mateus from Portugal) came in fancy clay "crock" bottles that were, at least, useful as inexpensive vases.

That, to our great benefit, is no longer the case. Winemakers near and far have gone to great lengths to provide us with "pink" wines that are more than just a pretty face, wines that have every bit of the sophistication and complexity as their red, white, and sparkling cousins.

The French, of course, have long led the way in this regard. Taste the wines of Tavel, the dry Rhône produced from Grenache and Cinsault grapes. The French are also fond of their rosés from Provence and the Loire Valley (Anjou). Or try some of the intriguing dry "blush" wines called *vin gris* (gray wine), like the one Santa Barbara's Richard Sanford produces from Pinot Noir. It's really just a light-styled red, with all the facets and embellishments of a fine red at a lower amplitude of color and body.

The most popular wine in the blush category is White Zinfandel, particularly that made at Sutter Home (20 million cases a year is not a figure to trifle with). That's partly because it's sweet and partly because the wine captures the bright cherry essence of the grape. Some of these *blanc de noir* wines show up under the name *oeil de perdrix* ("eye of the partridge").

Dry or sweet, most rosés are best consumed a bit chilled, and offer the perfect paradigm for "picnic." Nothing better, on a hot summer day, than a cold roast beef sandwich, a little potato salad, and a bottle or two of iced rosé. Or whatever menu suits your palate, and the wine, best.

Red Wines:

"The First Duty of a Wine is to be Red."

Red wines are the heart and soul of winedom. Why? Well, we are carnivores at base. We love meat, and particularly meat cooked over an open fire. That's why we are drawn to red wines aged in oak barrels, which confer a toasted, roasted character to wine. It is the allure of the camp fire, the allure of smoked meats, the allure of the post-prandial cigar. We are, of a sudden, back in the cave, roasting recently-hunted game. If the cave man had only had a glass of the Rhône (Syrah), he might not have been tempted by the suit, the tie, the office.

Red wines are the easiest wines to produce. You crush the grapes, and leave the juice in contact with the skins. The longer the skin contact, the greater the extraction of color, the greater the intensity of the wine. That's it.

Still, there is quite a range of weight and style. There are the Beaujolais wines, with their dainty, almost white-wine-like cherry fruitiness. These are light, almost ephemeral in weight, yet carry their own range of complexity and intrigue.

Pinot Noirs are the most alluring of red wines, this for their inherent sensuality. The best of these—be they grown in Burgundy or the cooler regions of California, Oregon, New Zealand, or Australia—are texturally sinful in their succulent, juicy, fleshy, near decadent attraction. They are the Holy Grail of winegrowing, because the Pinot is a difficult grape, in the vineyard, in the cellar, in the bottle, always promising one thing and delivering another.

The reds of Bordeaux (Cabernet Sauvignon and Merlot in the main) are intellectual creations, those of the Rhône (Syrah) and Tuscany (Sangiovese) cozy up to the fireplace, and the wild ones—Zinfandel and Barbera—provoke images of motorcycles and the wind in your hair. Something for everyone.

Dessert Wines:
For the Sweet Tooth in All of Us

The field of dessert wines is a cornucopia of riches, from low alcohol sipping Muscats (like Quady's "Electra") all the way up to the fully-fortified wines like Port and Sherry.

After dinner is a time to slow down and savor, and there's nothing better than a beguiling combination of sweets, solid, and liquid. My favorite dessert combination is as simple as a slice of honeydew melon coupled with a *botrytis*-influenced White Riesling or Sauvignon Blanc. The honied character of the wine sets off the melon so perfectly that you can easily make a case that heaven exists in the here and now. (I once wrote an article entitled "How to Spot an Alien," the thesis of which was that if someone did not like one of these silky sweet wines that was proof positive they were *not* from the third planet!)

These are fun wines, meant to be uncritically consumed and enjoyed. The Port with the cheddar. The Sherry with the biscuit. The Madeira with the cigar. The dried-berry recioto wines from Italy are in a category all their own, and even those low-alcohol spritzy sparklers produced from Muscat grapes serve only to prove the fullest extent of our imagination.

Some of these wines, particularly the botrytised Rieslings, can stand on their own as dessert, requiring no accompaniment whatever. The main thing, as always, is to try different wines, differing wine-food combinations, so as to discover what most appeals to your own personal palate. Every one of us has a different sense of what works and what doesn't, and discovering the limits of our sense of taste can be a real adventure, if only we playfully approach it in that manner.

Sparkling Wines:
A Little CO_2 Goes a Long Way

The range of sparkling wines is as diverse as that of literature. The lightweight Muscat or *crémant* spritzers are a lot like mystery stories, the dry rosés of champagne might remind you of Pat Conroy's work, while the full-throated, French bread-yeasty prestige cuvées can take you from Hemingway to Updike.

Just so, the vital, vivacious range of sparkling wine available today can take you from soup to nuts through a meal. It remains truly amazing that the sparkling wine producers of the world have yet to take a page out of the orange juice producers' handbook to come up with an ad along the lines of, "Sparkling Wine, It's Not Just for Weddings Anymore."

Thus we can draw from a wondrous array of *blanc de blancs* (a white wine produced solely from white grapes) for the appetizer course, perhaps a heftier, strawberry-laden blanc de noirs (a white, or "blush" wine made from red/black grapes) or even a robust red sparkler for the main course, and a *crémant* or a Muscat for the dessert course.

I remember tasting wines once with a 90-year-old Frenchman who attributed his good health and long life to a daily bottle of champagne. His trim fitness, his vigor, and vitality made it hard to argue against the notion. The thing to remember about sparkling wines is that they need not be relegated to what we euphemistically refer to as "special occasions." The idea to go away with here is to turn that notion sideways and take a proactive approach and make use of the magnificent selection of sparkling wines to create the occasion, to make it special by the way we approach it. Let the bubbles do their job, and let the good times flow!

HUMOR:
The Need to Laugh

Laughter is leavening, a vast relief valve from the pressures of modern day living. Wine, especially, requires Aristotle's "educated insolence" of wit to puncture the precocious, the pretentious, the pompous.

I remember the first time I saw a cork from Frog's Leap Winery (on the site of a farm that supplied San Francisco restaurants with frog's legs). It was printed with the slogan, "Time's fun when you're having flies." I howled.

In similar vein, there's a South African winery sporting a label "Goats do Roam," a light-hearted send-up of the French *Cotes du Rhône* wines. (To be fair, the guy's got goats on his property, okay?)

One group who always maniacally manifested a grand sense of perspective and balance was the gang at Sonoma's Gundlach-Bundschu, led by then-winemaker Lance Cutler and farmer-proprietor Jim Bundschu. Theirs was the masked crew that hilariously hijacked the Napa Valley Wine Train, substituting Sonoma Valley wines for those produced by the "Napkins." On another occasion, riding motorcycles and employing a helicopter—Lance wearing mask and cape—they seized a Napa-bound bus of wine writers and diverted it to their own winery "to cleanse their minds of Napa brainwashing."

Long time personal favorites are the famed "Lynch-Bob" cartoons, featuring the artistic flair of Bob Johnson and the dry, wry, biting wit of Mike Lynch (now a PR man, humor not paying all that well). A favorite showed a wine bar patron complaining of a red wine, "Geez, this wine is repulsive." Bartender: *The Wine Advisor* gave it a 96." Patron: "I'll take a case." Aieee!

French bistros are a natural setting for wine humor. One French tale has a Burgundian taking lunch, his faithful pooch at his side. When the sommelier asks for the old gentleman's wine preference, the Gaulish geezer says, "A glass of Chambertin for myself, and a little Beaune for my dog!"

Artist Ronald Searle brings a bit more edge to his wired and wonderful cartoons, the best of which depicted a wine delivery truck in flames, its tires flattened by huge tacks scattered across the road. The caption, "France: Annual Festival of Welcome to Italian Wines."

There was a story going around awhile back, perhaps apocryphal, of a wine writer constantly harassed by a marginal vintner to taste his wines. The guy finally corralled the scribe at a local restaurant, begged him to hold his seat while he scooted over to his nearby winery for a few bottles. While the vintner hovered, the poor fellow dutifully tasted the samples. Finally, forced by the hyperventilating vintner for an assessment, the writer intoned, "Don't travel well, do they?"

Which reminds me of my all-time favorite wine putdown. An Arkansas winemaker sent a sample of his best white wine to the state lab for analysis, and the report came back, "Your horse has diabetes." (Told to me as a true story by a most reputable source, a priest.)

Even my colleagues have a sense of the absurd about this unlikely profession. New Yorker Alexis Bespaloff once taped the following for his answering machine: "I'm not in right now, but if it's an emergency, white with fish and red with meat."

The trophy for the ultimate in wine pretension putdowns, however, remains with cartoonist James Thurber for his dinner host proclaiming over a raised glass, "It's a naïve domestic Burgundy without any breeding, but I think you'll be amused by its presumption."

Most memorable is our own self-mocking, from a position of strength, artfully exemplified by no less a personage than Robert Mondavi himself who, at nearly 90 years of age, showed up at Napa's prestigious wine auction dressed as Vanna White to pump up the volume. It doesn't get much better than that.

buying

Buying Wine:
Rule One (it's the only one), Get to Know Your Retailer

Next to your relationship with your psychiatrist—and a good butcher— getting to know your wine shop host will be your smartest, most helpful social connection in town. A good retailer, artfully tuning in to your particular tastes, as they evolve, will turn you toward wines that you might never have imagined trying, much less enjoying.

Retailers of today have grown past merely stacking boxes and ringing up sales. Many have newsletters to let customers in on special buys, offer basic wine education, and admit the rants and ramblings of the owner/editor. Randy Kemner of *The Wine Country* in Southern California and the folks at Schaefer's near Chicago—erudite and helpful—offer information that helps readers make better selections. Recall Justice Oliver Wendell Holmes' incisive dictum: "A mind expanded by a new idea never returns to its former size."

After helping customers learn to trust their own palate, the single greatest lesson you derive from a good retailer is that there is a plethora of tasty wine out there…that you can afford! It's true. You don't have to pay $100 a bottle to drink a great wine. There are wines out there with plenty of character, flavor, and varietal identity that sell for less than $15 the bottle.

How do you find them? You taste, and you taste, and you taste. You compare notes with your friends, with your retailer, and with your favorite restaurateur or wine waiter. Before you know it, you will have built up the confidence to trust your own palate. At that point you will have a leg up on those who remain cowed by what is nothing more than a bunch of grapes that got caught in a squeeze. Never let it out of your sight that what we're making all this fuss over is nothing more than the fermented juice of grapes!

Buying for Your Cache, Your Cellar

Whether you are buying wine to fill a six-bottle wine rack or a 6000-bottle underground cellar, it will be helpful to plan ahead a bit. The best way to do this is to work backwards from what your needs are. That way, when you're basting the roast for that elegant dinner party for the boss and her husband, you'll have just the wines you require, from soup to nuts.

The first thing to do, then, is to jot down a list of what wines you drink, first on a weekly basis, then planning ahead for a month, and then a year. If you've got a large Italian family that needs a bottle a night for your basic dinner, you're going to need at least 30 cases of wine to get you through the year...and that's not counting special events.

If, on the other hand, it's just you, and you're consuming a three- or four-ounce glass with dinner—which our cardiovascular experts now suggest as the basic minimum dosage to reduce heart risk up to 50 percent—then you will only require about four cases per year.

Most of us, naturally, fall somewhere in the middle of those parameters. We might be looking for some nice jug wine, or even a collapsible box wine, to get us through most evening meals. We're probably going to want to supplement our "daily bread" with something a bit nicer, what author Leon Adams used to refer to as "Sunday wine," for weekend dinners. And we're almost certainly going to want to step even that up a notch when we pull out all the stops to entertain our best friends or our colleagues from work.

It is for the last group that your cultivation of our ally, the retail shopkeeper, really pays dividends. Here is where you learn that special wines can be purchased for every course of your dinner party—from appetizer to main course, all the way through that extraordinary dessert you've picked out from the artisan bakery down the street—without requiring a home equity loan. Indeed, any experienced wine clerk ought to be able to find you taste-enhancing first course, main course, and dessert course wines—one bottle for each course—for less than $30 total. Is it a challenge? Yes. Is it doable? Double yes.

If you have storage room enough to buy wines by the case, I suggest an exercise that will expand your sensory awareness immensely. And it's fun, too. Buy one case of, say, a Pinot Noir that you really like, and two bottles of another Pinot from a different growing region. Taste the two wines at the outset of our little exercise, and jot down some notes on the two wines: How they are alike, and how they differ. Then continue to open bottles of the first wine over the course of the ensuing weeks. Get to know that wine intimately, so that it's almost as familiar to you as milk. Then, when you get to the last bottle of the case, taste that wine again with the second bottle of the other wine. I think you will be amazed at how noticeably *different* the two wines now appear to you, primarily because you've become so tuned into the first of them. You will surely see how important tasting experience is to the expansion of your wine knowledge.

Creating a "Cellar"... and Stocking It

Caring for a sound collection of wine is not half so difficult as creating the collection in the first instance. Sound cellaring requires little more than a dark place, a temperature that rarely varies more than five degrees on either side of the median, the absence of vibration—good wine cellars are rarely built beneath busy train tracks—and shelving suitable for storing.

Creating that sound collection is quite another story. It is not enough merely to amass some quantity of "bottled poetry" (Robert Louis Stevenson's apt phrase on a visit to Napa Valley more than a century ago) and store it in some dank, dark place. Clinically that is referred to as merely "a bunch of wine."

No, the true "cellar" is something pondered, weighed, considered, discussed, even deliberated. There is a strategy involved in creating a collection that is part passion and part cerebral.

The British, for example, go for the *glamour* cellar. When I say glamour, I'm talking about the wines the British wine trade made famous: Bordeaux, Port, Sherry. Englishmen are known to "lay down" a cellar, this having to do with putting bottles away for children, even for future grandchildren.

Modern day doctors, lawyers, and Silicon Valley whiz kids, on the other hand, tend to go for the *show* cellar. An interesting concept, but rather shameful in a way, since these glorious and expensive bottles of sunlight-plus-water are purchased more for prestige and for conspicuous display than for consumption. These wines end up being museum pieces, a thorough and complete waste according to my base and utilitarian nature.

The show cellar is exceeded in depravity only by the *investment* cellar, in which wines are purchased solely for their future economic value. Like the show cellar, this collection is rarely purchased for the wines themselves and what pleasure they might eventually give.

The *heritage* cellar is an offshoot the Brit's glamour cellar. Like the British, when we lay down wines for our children, we are at least understanding the collection as a living liquid meant to be consumed and enjoyed, if only at some later date.

Finally, there is what you might dub the *practical* cellar, wherein wines are ensconced wholly for the pure and unadulterated pleasure that they are expected to give.

If you choose to build and house a glamour collection, much like the investment cellar creator you are looking to pick the most highly-prized wines the world has to offer. Those you go for are the great French Bordeaux, rarely less than First Growths: Latour, Lafite, Petrus, and the like. And French Burgundies, beginning with Domaine de la Romanee Conti (at about a grand a bottle, newly released) and working your way down.

The glamour cellar would certainly contain some of world's greatest dessert wines, from French Sauternes to German *Auslesen*, from Hungarian Tokays to American Late Harvest Rieslings and Sauvignon Blancs. And, of course, Portuguese Ports of the ilk of Graham's and Warre's.

The show cellar would certainly have many of the same labels that show up in the glamour cellar, augmented by "name" California Cabernets, from Dunn to Diamond Creek, from Screaming Eagle to Heitz' Martha's Vineyard.

The investment cellar would combine, pretty much, the glamour and show cellars, looking for those wines which historically return big dividends on the capital initially invested. *The Wine Spectator* devotes a regular column on auction news, from the regular auction houses (Christie's and Sotheby's of London) to annual regional affairs, from Long Island to Napa and Sonoma. (Malcolm Forbes' son once laid out $156,450 for a flagon of 1787 Chateau Lafite Rothschild with the inscription "Th.J" on it. Yes, *that* Thomas Jefferson.)

I distinctly like the notion of the heritage cellar. This is almost exclusively because my twins—Curtis and Tamara—were born in one of California's most exquisite vintages, 1987, noted for wines with backbone, but also the meat to hold those bones together. The wines are accessibly fruity, but also have the structure to age well.

I save most of my glee for the practical cellar. Oh, sure, I have a few glamour wines (mostly Ports, given my Portuguese heritage), a couple of show wines (some DRC I traded for), a few investment wines, and the heritage wines for my kids. But most of my cellar is based on pragmatism, and that is what I wholeheartedly suggest to you. Base your cellar on what you eat and how you entertain, and you'll have a storehouse of pleasure that would put a sultan to shame.

Lay in a little sparkling wine for the aperitif course and the odd celebration now and again. You'll probably need less white wine than red, if only because most reds require some years of age before they are silky enough to be at their very best. I've given up on most California Chardonnays (too heavy, too oaky, too sweet) in favor of Sauvignon Blanc for mealtime use, though if you favor *al fresco* summertime dining you'll want to have some Chenin Blanc, White Riesling, or Gewürztraminer on hand.

On the red side, put Cabernets (French Bordeaux) down for aging—their tannins require a decade or more to soften sufficiently—and Pinot Noirs (French Burgundies) and Zinfandels down for more immediate use.

You'll want some wines to highlight those special desserts (Sauternes, Port, a Late Harvest Riesling) and even a rosé or two for frivolous, fun drinking.

The main thing in creating a collection is to cellar wines that you'll derive some pleasure from, whether that pleasure is the light in your children's eyes, an enhanced bank statement, or the pure sensual pleasure of a great Pinot Noir. Your call, of course.

Memoir: The First Time I Bought a Whole Case of Wine

The first time I girded up my courage to buy a full case of wine was in the summer of 1972. I had been working in a San Francisco wine shop while attending law school, and the owner had given me a bottle of 1964 Beaulieu Vineyard Georges de Latour Private Reserve the previous Christmas. It had seemed to be pretty good stuff.

Even then Beaulieu was allocating the Private Reserve, which meant that one could only purchase six bottles of the precious fluid at a time. If one were alone, that is, and not bent on subterfuge. And a little lucky. As it happened, twice within a period of three weeks from the day the '68 Private Reserve was released it just happened that my work took me to the sleepy little hamlet of Rutherford. (You think it was a coincidence that the first expensive bottle of wine I ever bought also sported the name Latour? Chateau Latour? A chess player, I liked the castle/rook on the label!)

On the first occasion a friend was traveling with me. John had just returned from Malaysia, where he had been teaching science with the Peace Corps, and had brought one of his students back to be his wife. He had no interest in wine at all, his mind being otherwise occupied, so through his agency I was able to secure a full case of this rare wine. On the second occasion it was my father who was along to provide a body to secure the second half of my second case of this great wine.

You have to understand the near-Scottish thinking that went into this. I had a hunch that this was going to turn into a moderately valuable wine. At $5.25 per bottle, those two cases set me back $132.32, which was then a full week's wages! [A couple of cases today will set you back more than two grand!] But I had a plan. Eventually, I reasoned, this wine would double in value and I could sell one case and drink the other for free. A month after I had secured my two cases, the winery raised the price to $5.65 per bottle. Ha! I was already on my way!!

But there was one factor that I hadn't taken into account. The wine itself. The rich, green olive, herbaceous fruit. The texture that, with age, rounded out into a silky, supple, mouthwatering jewel that made my poor attempts at culinary expertise glow. In a word, the wine was too bloody good to sell. Indeed, over the period of nearly two decades that I drank—and immensely enjoyed that wine—only a single bottle was not uncorked at our dinner parties. (A gift to a winemaker friend on his wedding.) Even when the auction value of the '68 punched through $200 a bottle, I never had the slightest thought of relinquishing more than that single bottle... for any price.

As it happened, I moved from wine shop clerk to tasting room host and tour guide at Sebastiani Vineyards two months after making my grand purchase. Shortly after that I began a career writing about wines. It didn't take me long to recognize just how valuable and exquisite BV's '68 Private Reserve was. Beaulieu's late winemaster Andre Tchelistcheff—I dubbed him The Russian Leprechaun—told me that it was the finest Napa Valley Cabernet in his considerable memory.

When my wife and I finally drank our last bottle some years ago, the only thing I could think of was: Why hadn't I bought three cases?!

The Curse of Corks...
and How to Get Past Them

Entrance to the Kingdom comes at a price, most often strength and dexterity combined. Gaining entrance to the package is the single worst thing about wine. Why, for goodness' sake, do we make it so difficult?

The cork is all about tradition, and it is a fine one. Cork has protected the fine wines of the world for centuries. (Understand too, I'm part Portuguese, and most of the best corks come from "cork oak" trees grown in Portugal. The cork can only be "harvested" once every nine years.) There is a certain elegance to an artfully drawn cork, even if it's plastic.

That said, it is thoroughly embarrassing to pull a corkscrew and come up with nothing more than crumbled cork, or draw the danged thing so hard that red wine meets white shirt. The hard reality is that cork demands an implement that is awkward to operate, the corkscrew. The tried-and-true waiter's corkscrew is the easiest for most of us to use, but make sure yours has a helical screw (like "The Rabbit™!" and not an auger [augers can shred soft cork]). The tined "Ah-So™!" is easy for some, but that also requires a bit of hand strength. I'm not a fan of the pressure-operated cork pullers, but they're more comfortable for some folk.

Innovative packaging is beginning to come into play here. Bag-in-box is terrific for everyday wines, nearly eliminating spoilage problems. There's a new "screw cork" that is of interest. Metal screw caps may eventually surpass, or even eliminate corks. The screw cap seems to preserve wine as well or better than the cork, and it is certainly easier to open. As much as we love the tradition of the cork, it is essential that wine be more accessible if its popularity is ever to become universal, as this civilizing beverage certainly deserves.

tasting

The "Tastes" of Wine:
What's that Bell Pepper Doing in My Glass?

I still remember when I first learned that flavors had chemical underpinnings. It had to do with Cabernet Sauvignon and its oft comparison to bell peppers, particularly when the grapes are grown in a cool area, like California's Monterey County. What I learned was that bell pepper has a chemical signature: Di-methoxy tri-isobutyl-pyrazine. For years after, I could rattle that off as easily as my own name. Say it a few times. It does have a ring to it.

That doesn't mean that you could dilute a bit of the DTBP in a glass of water and it would taste like Cabernet. What it does mean is that foods and beverages have identifiable, replicable flavors. What it ought to mean is that wine writers ought to stick with flavors people can understand (apple, for example, is Ethyl-2-methyl butyrate), rather than falling back on "rich and full-bodied" (which says exactly what?) or "prismatic luminescence" (uh huh). Remember grape Kool Aid? Methyl anthranilate.

What's really fascinating is that our noses are extraordinary at picking out these flavors, even at spectacularly low concentrations. Did you know that your nose can detect bell pepper's pungent presence at 0.02 parts per billion? I'm told that's the equivalent of about one drop in your average municipal swimming pool. If the chlorine level is low.

Here are some of the more common tendencies: Chardonnay (apple or lemon), White Riesling (apricot), Sauvignon Blanc (freshly-cut grass), Cabernet Sauvignon (bell pepper or cassis), Pinot Noir (black cherry), Zinfandel (raspberry), Sangiovese (strawberry). But every wine has its own signature, and often that signature has more than one aspect. The fun lies in nosing them out into the open…and enjoying the mix of flavors.

How to Taste (and Mostly *Smell*) Wine

One of the nasty icons we must destroy is the nonsense of 100-point valuation systems (more on this in a minute). Not only do these pervasive, prevailing scoring systems reduce the ineffability of wine's highly subjective and artistic beauty to cold, objective numbers, but they diminish the enduring sense of wine's individuality, both in its presentation and in its acceptance by you, the wine's audience. My personal counter is embodied by Hinkle's First Wine Law which, as you know, says, "There are only three categories of wine: 1) I like it; 2) I don't like it; and 3) I'll drink it if someone else pays for it!" That's something we can all understand.

The physical act of tasting wine is actually one of smelling wine. When we talk of taste, we are talking about the tongue, which reacts to a half dozen sensations: Sweet, sour, salt, bitter, astringent, and a new one, *umami* (that full, rich sense of deliciousness recently discovered by Japanese researchers). Fairly limiting, wouldn't you say?

But when you examine the range of smell—which accounts for fully 90 percent of what we call "taste"—we're talking six to 10...1000! That's right, up to 10,000 identifiable sensations, from apricot (White Riesling) to black cherry and rose petal and rare filet mignon (Pinot Noir). The range is astonishing, almost beyond credulity. But these are real, replicable descriptors that help us to understand a wine far better than the nebulous "rich and full" or the ridiculous "prismatic luminescence."

Curiously, we once thought that female tasters had inherently better palates, but a closer look demonstrated that they had a better sensory vocabulary (for having spent more time in the kitchen). Experience counts.

As always, the best rule of thumb is to trust your own palate over that of others. Or, if you prefer pathetic puns, "No nose knows like your nose knows."

Scoring Systems:
and Why I Don't Recommend Them

There is a value to numbered scoring systems, but it is limited. When you're first learning to taste wine critically, it can be helpful to break down wines by category, and even assign numbers to those categories. The U.C. Davis 20-point scale *deconstructs* each wine by color and clarity, aroma and bouquet, acidity and sweetness, body and texture, flavor and overall quality. This can be useful at the outset, when you don't yet have the confidence to assess each wine as an integrated whole.

Here's the problem: You can break down a funky, herbaceous Pinot Noir, deducting points for "flaws" right on down the line… and it can be thoroughly wonderful to drink. Or, you can take a "clean" white wine, *sans* obvious flaws, and tote up a high score. At worst you could have a 13-point Pinot Noir and a 17-point white wine…and the former would be the far better wine.

The other problem with wine magazines and their 100-point systems is that they perpetuate the "guru" status of the taster and the acolyte status of the reader. I much prefer *Quarterly Review of Wine's* approach, giving accurate descriptions of the wines in lieu of points. "We want the reader to participate in assessing the wines we review," says founder/publisher Richard Elia. "If we give our readers enough information, they'll have a pretty good idea as to whether or not they'll like any given wine."

I agree with Elia. The bottom line is that empowered consumers are better, far more informed consumers than those blindly working off of someone else's palate. The fact that I like a given wine offers little indication as to whether or not you'll like it. You've got to taste it for yourself to find that out.

The U. C. Davis 20-Point Scoring System:
Useful as a guide

Here's the wine college's 20-point scoring system in chart form. It remains useful in a "what to look for" sense, rather than in any literal sense, where it really allows for (indeed, almost encourages) a distortion of values.

Appearance (cloudy, clear, brilliant)	2 points
Color (off, correct)	2 points
Aroma/Bouquet (off/true)	4 points
Vinegar (yes/no)	2 points
Total Acidity (low/high/appropriate)	2 points
Sweetness (as appropriate)	1 point
Body (as appropriate)	1 point
Flavor (abnormal, desirable)	2 points
Bitterness/Astringency (as appropriate)	2 points
General Quality (the "fudge" factor)	2 points

The point, here, is that I am willing to overlook minor flaws—cloudiness, a color that isn't ideal—when a wine really shows up where it counts most, flavor and texture. When I'm rating wines for columns and articles, I use what is essentially a five-point system that is weighted towards the favorable end of the scale: Excellent, Very Good, Good, Fair (i.e. commercially acceptable), Poor (obviously flawed). When I need a little leeway and fine-tuning, this can easily be expanded to a 15-point scale by adding pluses and minuses. It's all according to what your needs are.

Comparative Tasting:
The Appreciation of Difference

The comparative tastings you hear the most about are wine judgings, the competitions where a gold medal is money in the bank and a silver or bronze is a sisterly kiss. Wine judgings are best for those of us who do the judging: We get to taste a lot of wines…and someone else has to wash the glasses.

You can gain greater benefits of comparative tastings at home. Simply tasting two different Chardonnays—saying "I like this one better than that one"—is instructive. The triangle tasting helps you to spot similarities and differences. Pour two glasses of one wine and a single glass of another, placing a sticky label on the bottom of each glass to identify which wine it is (so you can't see the name). Move the glasses about so that you don't know which is which, then taste each one to see if you can spot the one that is different. An excellent beginning exercise.

Regional tastings can be quite enlightening. You might compare Merlot-based wines from France (Bordeaux), Napa Valley, Sonoma County, Washington State, and Australia…and be startled at the differences (and similarities). Vertical tastings are also intriguing, tasting the same wine from the same winery through a series of vintages. You'll be able to note the winery's "style," yet find differences from one year to the next.

Recall my favorite comparative technique: Buy two bottles of one Pinot Noir and a case of another, tasting one against the other at the outset, then only tasting daily from the case (for weeks) until you get to the last bottle. Then compare it with the other bottle of the second wine. By getting to really *know* the one wine, it will really stand out in the final tasting.

The Technique of Tasting

Tasting wine—mostly *smelling* wine, as we have discussed—is about putting all of our senses to work. If you count the satisfying "thunk" of a cork popping out of the bottle, you use every one of your five senses to fully appreciate wine.

So, after our sense of hearing, we next put our sense of sight into play. What is the wine's color? A white wine should show a range from near clear to rich, buttery yellow, reds cherry to plum. Brown tinges imply oxidation. The wine should also be fairly clear, without cloudiness.

Then we *smell*. This is our focal point. Is the fruit fresh, bright, brisk, and inviting? Or are there stale or moldy smells that are off-putting, that do not invite a meal, a snack? That would be a major problem. The best wines make our mouth water for something equally tasty.

When we put wine in our mouth, we do taste the wine. Is the sweetness appropriate? Are tannins and acidity in balance? Texture becomes a big part of our wine experience. We call this "mouth feel." Good Pinot Noirs have a succulent, juicy, sensual texture that is just this side of sinful. Sauvignon Blancs, when they are young, often have a hard, mineral quality that turns oily and rich with time in bottle.

You've seen serious tasters swirl the wine in the glass. This exposes the wine to oxygen, which releases flavor components into the air, the better for you to smell the wine. That's also why tasters draw air over the tongue, to further release flavor esters into their nasal passages.

What of spitting? Well, unless you're tasting a dozen wines, it's probably not necessary. But do think designated driver if you're on the road. Wine folk are responsible folk, after all.

The Flavors of Wine:
Varietal Characteristics

The essence of our love of wine is that each grape variety brings a different flavor profile to the table. If that were not so, we'd be stuck with the grape equivalent of milk. Healthful, but very boring.

But wine is breathtaking with its worldwide range of flavors. Take White Riesling. Whether it is grown in Germany or in the Finger Lakes (New York), if the climate is cool enough the wine scintillates with apricot purity. Sauvignon Blanc, on the other hand, grown in a cool climate comes at you with a brisk bell pepper, green bean, and tobacco character; in a warmer location is more honeydew melon-like.

Chenin Blanc has a floral essence, while Chardonnay can be all over the map—it's a winemaker's wine, it's so malleable—from crisp grapefruit and mineral-driven in a Chablis climate to broad, with butter and apple in a warmer climate. Gewürztraminer is what its name says it is, spicy (nutmeg, cinnamon) and alive.

The same thing happens with reds, Cabernet Sauvignon in particular. In a cool climate, herbaceous characteristics show up: bell pepper, green bean, and tobacco (yes, it's related to Sauvignon Blanc). In a warm climate, the wine has more cassis, black currant, and blackberry fruit. Zinfandel? Raspberry. Syrah/Shiraz? Strawberry.

And then there's Pinot Noir. Cold climate, it's black cherry and rose petal; warmer climate it's strawberry jam and clove spiciness.

Don't forget the dessert wines, from Sherry's nutty notes to Port's plum, to the botrytised wines' rich honey. The range is vibrantly exhaustive and exhilarating. Hey, that's the point of it, and the fun of it. Wallow in the wondrous immensity of wine's range. There is something in this liquid magic to please every taste under the sun. That is the ultimate art of wine.

A Word about Wine Writers and Wine Magazines

Okay, maybe a few words, "grain of salt." As in, don't take what you read too awfully seriously. Be skeptical—not cynical—don't be afraid to question what you read, what you hear. Don't be afraid to filter things through your own experience, your own palate.

Wine has, over the years, become an increasing part of the Wednesday "Food Page" in your local newspaper. That's good, up to the point where those columns offer information, education, enlightenment. That's not so good when they offer only self-anointed gurus plugging themselves. Be wary of the self-centered, the self-congratulatory.

The good news is there is more information out there than there ever has been before, and to the degree that it helps you, the reader, to stand on your own two feet, to create and understand your own likes and dislikes, then it is beneficial. Like one of my favorite colleagues, Bob Thompson, I've always felt that my job, as a wine writer, was to write myself out of a job, to create a readership of individuals who can make their own choices, and defend those choices actively against those who push for any sort of consensus. Consensus, when it comes to art, pulls all of us down to the lowest, basest common denominator, lessening each and every one of us.

When it comes to wine writers, I commend to your attention someone who describes wines rather than judges them (affixing dehumanizing "points" to each wine). What is most useful to you is a clear, competent, complete assessment of a wine's qualities…upon which you can base your own ultimate judgment. Example A: "This Cabernet is the best I've ever had, rich, bold, and scintillating." Example B: "This Cabernet shows cassis and iodine fruit, framed artfully with toasted French bread oak; juicy, supple texture; long finish; filet mignon, anyone?" Which one of those tells you what the wine tastes like? Which one tells you what sort of food it might be best with? Which helps you to say, "This one appeals to [doesn't appeal to] my palate"?

Find a writer who, like Roger Ebert for film, is passionate about what he or she does, and offers a probing, incisive, and insightful understanding of what's going on with the wine. For that reason, I favor a Robert M. Parker Jr. [*The Wine Advocate*], say, over any magazine's panel. However expert the panelists are—and they are often very good at what they do—you can usefully work from an individual's comments far more easily. You see, once you understand Parker's personal bias toward bold, ripe, masculine, oak-laden, "statement" wines, it is easy to handicap his input, it is easy to interpolate from his palate to yours, even if yours is quite different. There's no way to figure the bias of any panel's consensus, no matter how good its individuals are. Thus, I can tell, from an Ebert review, whether or not I'll like the movie with a high degree of accuracy; I can tell, from a Parker assessment, whether or not I am likely to appreciate a given wine. The information I have received has been useful.

A Confusion of Stemware:
The Right Glass for the Right Wine

As you are learning, wine is an incredibly sensory experience. The more senses we can entice, the more entrancing our experience…and our memory of it.

So, in selecting a glass for all purpose usage—more on the stylish glassware later—we are looking for a clear, thin-walled glass that allows full appreciation of the visual sensations of the wine, from the straw-yellow-gold spectrum of white wines through the ruby-garnet-brick range of hues found among the reds.

You want a glass whose capacity is large enough that, half-filled, it holds a standard serving portion. While most wine books suggest that an eight or nine-ounce glass is sufficient, I strongly hold out for a 12-ounce minimum size, especially for red wines, where you want the portion size to be at least six ounces.

I say "half-filled" because you want an ample empty upper portion of the glass to enfold the aromas volatilized by gentle swirling action. (To swirl your glass without spilling or sloshing, turn a tight, one- to two-inch circle with the stem of the glass.) Our sense of smell is the crux of wine appreciation, the very basis of our accurate and complete understanding of any given wine. The size and shape of the glass influences aromatics capture and, to be honest, you want a glass large enough to allow you to insert your schnoz completely without risk of dampening it or your enthusiasm! (Which means that saucer-shaped Champagne glasses are best broken in the fireplace. Flutes are immeasurably better for the bubbly.)

Master Austrian glassmaker Georg Riedel has clearly demonstrated that the shape of the glass affects the actual taste of the wine, as well as the tactile sensation of the wine cascading about our tongue and palate. The texture of wine, from coarse and tannic to supple and silky, is an equally important part of our sensory equation.

The sense of sound comes into play if you add in the musical "clink" of toasting and Georg's "murmuring of the wine in the glass," not to mention the satisfying "thwup" of a cork being drawn and the disconcerting slurping sound of air being drawn in over the wine in your mouth (the latter dramatically increases aroma volatilization). Maybe the most satisfying aural

imprint remains that long, low, sighed "Ahhh!" that tells us the wine found its way into our very being by provoking wondrous sensory responses. See Hinkle's Second Law (on page 86), which explains the vibrant sensuality of superb Pinot Noirs and French Burgundies: "Great Pinot Noir inspires one to create new sins…and wish to commit them!" Yes, even glassware can evoke the sensualist in us.

Though a standard 12-ounce glass might be sufficient for 95 percent of our needs, try the 20-ounce glassware designed to showcase Cabernet Sauvignon, and especially Riedel's 24-ounce Burgundy glass—it can hold a whole bottle of wine—that exquisitely shows off every last ounce of Pinot Noir's succulent, juicy, decadent, sinuous sensuality.

As Georg Riedel reminds us, "The glass is the last link in the chain of vineyard to barrel to bottle to consumer. Wines have greatly individualistic characters, so it seems foolish to think that we can show every wine at its best in the same shape or size of glass." Thus, though we might well be able to drink any wine in any glass, to truly and comprehensively appreciate a wine of distinction, definition and personality, there is wisdom in paying attention to the stemware in which we showcase our favorite wines.

pairings

Table Settings:
It's not Just a Tablecloth and Four Forks

Great pleasure can be derived from setting a fancy table, with all the requisite bells and whistles (read "four forks"). It is truly impressive to sit down to a full-dress table setting that allows a meal to unfold in the manner of a flower petal opening to ballet music in superb slow-motion photography. I remember a most spectacular meal, served at the fabulous Die Ente Restaurant in Frankfurt one evening: Seven courses (small portions) and 21 wines (small "tastes") served over a four-hour period. Just the right pace for the exquisite meal.

Equal pleasure can also be obtained from just one each of the silverware, plates, and stemware, and just one to three wines: aperitif, main course, and dessert. Grace is attainable in even the simplest of presentations.

Table settings need not be difficult. Napkin and fork are placed to the left of the plate, while knife and spoon go to the right. The blade of the knife faces in, toward the plate. The water glass sits at the head of the plate, left of center. The wine glass is to the right of center. That's it.

Yes, you can go much fancier, and that can be fun, adding extra forks (for the salad course, dessert, and such). And extra wine glasses. When you have more than one, pour from left to right so that people can remember which wine is which.

While there can be different wine glasses for different wine types, as you have just seen, a basic 12-ounce glass is sufficient for most dining experiences. The primary thing to keep in mind is that we don't want to intimidate our guests, with wine, with food, with mind-numbing place settings. Relax a little, cut the rules back a bit, and aim for comfortable.

Wine and Food Pairing:
Have a Little Fun with It

The old rules are out. "White with fish, red with meat" worked as a place to start, but too many folk made them absolutes and, as we know, absence of variation only reaps boredom.

There is nothing dull about approaching wine and food pairings playfully. I start—and occasionally end—most discussions with, "Pinot Noir goes with everything." That is the easy way out, because great Pinot Noirs are so soft and succulently juicy that they can bend to most foodstuffs, from spicy Thai and Mexican to rich meats and savories.

If you must have rules, play the contrast and complement card. But even that allows lots of leeway for an adventuresome spirit, and that's what we want working for us. The notion of contrast is that we want the wine to go against the nature of the food. If, as example, we're serving something bland, then spice it up with the wine: Gewürztraminer is spicy and saucy by nature, and will make any simple food taste that much better.

Complement is just what it says it is: We're working to have the wine complement the food. Thus, we want a wine of similar size and weight to the dish we're serving. If we're talking a rich, sweet dessert, we want a rich, sweet wine, like a late harvest wine with *botrytis*, like the French Sauternes (Chateau d'Yquem and the like).

True fun is working against type. Take Sauternes, that beguilingly rich, sweet beauty. Normally you serve that with something equally sweet, or in contrast with *fois gras*. But I remember being utterly bowled over when French hosts once served a great Sauternes with roasted chicken…an amazingly delicious combination.

So, our rule of thumb is this: Approach wine and food pairings like you do sex, with a playfully open and adventuresome attitude, and prepare to be amused, amazed, and completely contented.

Wine and Music Pairings

The wine-and-food-pairing gag has finally run to full circle. We have progressed (and regressed) from the primitive notion "white with fish, red with meat" to the *advanced* anarchy that pervades today ("any wine, any food"). Which works only if you're starting with a supple, sulky, sullen, silken Pinot Noir.

Always searching for something new upon which to hang their vinous *chapeaux*, American vintners are now playing the "what wine with which music" game. This is a new parlor pairings gambit in which consumers and critics are invited to guess whether sparkling wine (*Champagne*, if you are dyed-in-the-*laine* French) is better accompanied by grand opera or some sort of fizzy electronic composition.

This *nouveau* slant was started by Napa Valley's Franciscan Vineyards awhile back when they released samples of their latest Oakville Estate Bordeaux-blend red, Magnificat, with CDs of Johann Sebastian Bach's...uh huh, *Magnificat*. What maintained the clever connection, of course, was that the wine, a magnificently complex and layered vinous creation, was clearly mirrored in Bach's own—well—complex and layered musical creation.

In the pairing game—be it wine-and-food or wine-and-music—we call this *complement*. As opposed, natch, to *contrast*. Which, in this case, would be to match Magnificat (the wine) with something obvious, almost bawdy. Ice-T, or something country-and-western?

Winemaker/parachutist/ballet dancer Don Blackburn (formerly of Byington Winery) uses musical analogies in educational tastings. He'll pour a light, fruity *Nouveau* Beaujolais, a velvety Pinot Noir, and a firmly-structured Cabernet. After the wines have been tasted, students are then asked to match the wines up to three musical offerings, usually, Don says, "a silly little Mozart divertimento, a Hayden piece full of French horns, and the heavyweight opera *Carmina Burana*." Nearly all would feel most comfortable with Mozart and the Nouveau, the Cab with *Carmina*. "If there was any confusion," he adds, "we'd taste the Beaujolais while listening to the opera, which obviously doesn't mesh much. I mean it's ugly!"

The complementary match-ups can be fairly obvious. The wild spiciness of a California Zinfandel snuggles up cozily with almost any C&W "she done me wrong" song, anything that carries a title like *My Wife Ran Off with My Best Friend*, and *I Sure Do Miss Him*.

Where florid, over-oaked, high alcohol California Chardonnays would certainly require something bombastic and overstated—some state song, perhaps?—a French Chablis (also Chardonnay, but lean, green, and crisp) might be more comfortable with something delicate that features piccolos and flutes.

Merlot is all the rage these days, from Sonoma Valley to St. Emilion. This soft and silky, velvet-textured red likely requires the velvet tones of a clarinet. (Does this whole thing come to a head when restaurants will feature mood music to match their featured wines?)

The great outlaw wine, Gewürztraminer—outcast only because people are leery of trying to pronounce it (try ghah-vertz'-trah-mee'-naihr)—with its naturally frivolous spiciness, would pair up nicely with anything from hipster rap to Stravinsky's *The Rite of Spring*.

Which brings us, inevitably, to Pinot Noir/French Burgundy. When you revert to the old sensory descriptors, you note that virtually all that are employed for the grand Pinot are sensual terms, from supple to silky, from decadent to delicious and on to redolent, and just plain sexy. So, we're agreed, eh? It's Ravel's *Bolero*. Or a good strip tease accompaniment.

The main thing is to take the same tack in matching wine with music as you do when matching wine with food: Be playful, be adventuresome, don't be bound by "rules," and keep a healthy sense of humor handy for those instances where the match-up falls flatter than a minor chord in the divertimento.

Interlude:
A Musing on the Nature of Wine

Why does wine even exist? It's a fair question. If it were only for the fact of its being alcohol-preserved grape juice, would that be enough? I don't think so. It would simply be another commodity beverage, much like milk or orange juice, perhaps slightly more regarded for the health benefits conferred solely by the presence of alcohol.

What begins to set wine apart is that particular places of origin can show themselves all the way through to the finished product. (We'll talk more about this idea of "appellation" in the next segment.) Yes, Idaho potatoes are pretty good, and Florida orange juice is sweet and tasty, but could they be consistently identified as such in a blind taste test? (Please do not write if the answer to that is "yes." I don't really want to know.)

But even beyond this fascinating concept of "personality of place" is the still more intriguing aspect of wine's "civilizing" properties. Think about it. Wine is a social beverage. Wine brings people together. Wine draws out the most essential flavors of food. Wine seems to enhance the content and quality of our conversation. Wine even has spiritual qualities that range far beyond the biblical "Miracle of Cana."

Wine is the liquid food that allows innovative chefs an additional "food color" to work with from their food *palette* as they create the artistic culinary masterpieces they are known for.

All this from the humble grape, this simple agricultural product that so enlivens our mealtime pleasures. Gives you a little something to think about the next time you draw the cork from your favorite bottle of Gewürztraminer, Zinfandel, or Pinot Noir.

winegrowing

The Appellation Trap:
What it Means; What it Doesn't Mean

There is much to make of "appellations," the specific sites where wines of personality, wines of specific identity are *grown*. It is this anthropomorphic aspect of wine that sets it apart from every other beverage, because Burgundian Pinot Noir grown in Gevrey Chambertain is distinctively different from Pinot Noir grown in Volnay, because Cabernet Sauvignon (Bordeaux) grown in Pauillac shows violets while the same grape grown in Rutherford often reminds first of green olives.

The problem is this: Because certain famed sites so forcefully demonstrate this wondrous "personality of place," we want appellations to be statements of *quality* when, in fact, they are merely statements of *geography*. At best, of course, they are profoundly personal statements of geography.

Appellations can never be statements of quality because any appellation is only as good as the worst producer allowed its use, and because even the finest appellations—supported by so-called "quality assurances"—can never exceed their least conscientious member. (When, for example, certain appellations within Bordeaux limited those name uses to wines produced at or less than 35 hectoliters per hectare (hl/ha), that law did not limit vineyard production to 35 hl/ha across the board: It merely insured that the *first 35 hl/ha* went into wines given that particular appellation within Bordeaux. The portion of production above 35 hl/ha simply received a lesser *"vin du pays"* ["country wine"] designation.)

If you, as a consumer, want a quality statement from the label, it has to be the name of the producer, the reputation he or she has built over the years. Most of us can name one or two producers whose wines we "know" to be good, even though we've never tasted a given wine. Definitive clues as to quality cannot be derived solely from a wine's appellation.

The Winemaker:
Alchemist or Babysitter?

Having just suggested to you that producer (and, by inference, winemaker) is more important than appellation in terms of drawing a quality statement from any label, I'm going to toss one more monkey wrench into the cogs: The best winemakers will freely admit that it's really the grape grower who determines the quality of the wines they tend in their cellars.

Listen to the words of the late Andre Tchelistcheff, who put Napa Valley Cabernet Sauvignon on the map with the legendary wines he "made" for Beaulieu Vineyard for nearly four decades: "The most important signs in a vineyard are the footprints of the winemaker." Like most great winemakers, Andre would tell you that by the time the grapes hit the crusher, 85 to 90 percent of what could have been done or not done to influence the quality of the wine…has either been done or not done!

There was a time—in the 1980s—when one of my favorite winemakers wore shirts open nearly to his navel and sported gold chains around his neck. He had fully invested himself in the notion of "winemaker as alchemist." But reality soon set in, and he regained the modesty of one who knows that great wines can only be produced from superior grapes. It doesn't work the other way around. Bad grapes, bad wines.

Brother Timothy, when he was winemaster for Christian Brothers Wines, told me that a winemaker was essentially a babysitter. "A constructive babysitter," he added.

Memoir:
Hinkle's Laws

It may have escaped your attention, but wine is getting more than a skoshe too precious, more than a mite too complicated these days. Wine has evolved to the point where doctoral dissertations are written over the distinctions between various clones of, say, Pinot Noir grapes. Not only that, but consumers are so confused and beguiled that they are only now learning that Zinfandel can be red! Imagine that. Comes in *two* colors! (Okay, three if you count rosés.)

Thirty years ago I worked as a tour guide at a Sonoma Valley winery. Prior to the tour, if the weather was nice during the late summer, I'd take my group across the street from the tasting room to the edge of one of the winery's vineyards. "Let me explain how wine is made," I'd say, picking a cluster of grapes. "You crush the grapes in your hands, wait patiently for five days…and it's wine! Any questions?" (Try and explain the production of beer that simply. Can't be done. Wort, woofer, tweeter…tough.)

Sadly, due to what seems to be a conspiracy of pretentiousness from some of my colleagues—led by what I call the "prismatic luminescence" school of wine writing—we seem to be swamped in ostentation and grandiosity. Fortunately, Hinkle's Laws form a formidable breakwater against the tsunami of overwhelming and pride-filled preciousness. Better still, none of these "laws" will insist that you need 14 different sets of crystal in order to enjoy that number of different wine types.

Hinkle's First Law: "There are only three categories of wine: 1) I like it; 2) I don't like it; and 3) I'll drink it if someone else pays for it!" The genesis of the first law has to do with the utter silliness of invoking 100-point scales to judge and categorize wine quality. As if the fermented juice of ripe grapes could be reduced to such cold, numerical enumeration. Bah and humbug. Great and complex wines, like refined and cultivated folk, possess qualities so diverse and so wondrous that even a 1000-point scale would not do them justice. Instead, we are best reduced to language which culminates, with the very best of the world's wines, with the likes of "oooh" and "ahhh," and the ever popular "wow!"

Hinkle's Second Law: "Great Pinot Noir inspires one to create new sins…and wish to commit them!" Mere numbers are especially incapable of describing the wholly sensual textural qualities of the finest French Burgundies and scintillating California and Oregon Pinots. We use words like *succulent* and *juicy*, *fleshy* and *decadent*, but even these only scratch the surface of the hedonistic nature of these extraordinary, ambrosially bawdy delights. They must be tasted, touched, felt, and savored before one truly understands and appreciates the innate sensuality of artfully grown, craftily made Pinot Noir.

The French, in their ever wondrous display of sensual vocabulary, immediately hew to feminine analogies when rhapsodizing over the textural delights of the red Burgundy. They even draw upon religious icons, suggesting that a fine Burgundy "slides down your throat like the good Lord Jesus in silk trousers." Hey, they're French. If they can get away with that, even in these politically correct times, more power to 'em.

Hinkle's Fourth Law: (In the Jeopardy format) "Answer: Gewürztraminer! Question: What do you say when someone sneezes?" The theory, of course, is that anybody who can twirl their tongue around *gesundheit* correctly can certainly master "ghah-vertz'-trah-mee'-naihr." (Maybe if you blurt it out quickly. Go on, try it!) The Gewürz is, of course, that spicy, delicately floral white wine in dire danger of dying out if we don't learn how to pronounce it soon enough to order a bottle before it's all gone. (If you're wondering, Hinkle's Third Wine Law isn't much, I'm not proud of it, so there's no need to repeat it here.)

Hinkle's Fifth Wine Law: "It is better to suffer with wine than to suffer without wine." This is not to enter into the great philosophical debate on the ennobling qualities of suffering. No, the notion really points to the idea that, when faced with the absolute and irrevocable necessity of enduring evil and its offshoots, you may as well temper the experience with a glass of the bubbly, a goblet of the Gewürz, a tumbler of the Pinot, a thimble or three of the Port. Unless you're into enhancing your pain through masochism—I'm making no judgment here, one way or the other—it just seems sensible to put the pain in perspective with a judicious dose of Nature's own best medicine. (Perhaps this one might better be stated, "A burger with Beaujolais is better than filet mignon with water." What do you think?)

I was thinking of coming up with a sixth law, but there's not much point in trying to make something simple if you're just going to work your way around to complicating it again. Still, I've always been intrigued by the incipient humor in collective nouns, as applied to wine. If it's a gaggle of geese, is it "a murder of Merlots?" A pride of Pinots? A rafter of Rieslings? A flock of Fumés? A covey of Cabernets? A zoo of Zinfandels? (Blurt it out! Quickly!) A gaggle of Gewürzes? Is there a sixth law in there somewhere? Beats me.

The Seasons of Wine:

Like the Sun, Hate the Rain...In the Summer

After a time of winter repose—when vines rest in their dormancy—the spring leaps out upon us and the vines come roaring back to life. Mustard plants, brilliantly yellow, carpet the forest-green vine rows. From the moment of bud break, frost protection is vital lest tender shoots become blackened and burnt. Mildew must be monitored, pests must be countered, and vine growth must be kept on an even keel.

The most important aspect of winegrowing is that our sites are chosen well. Summer days must be warm enough for sugar and character development, while evenings must be cool enough to allow ripening grapes to retain natural acidity sufficient to literally "frame" fruit identity, to push it forward. Growers like the sun, but wish the rain away in summer. Let it fall in the winter, as it does so conveniently in places like southern Europe and California. Ah, the benefits of a two-season Mediterranean climate.

Comes the fall, vineyards are plush with fruit and all attentions are focused on harvesting grapes at their optimum maturity. The best winemakers spend long hours in the field, checking day-by-day conditions of each grape variety, most effectively by literally tasting individual grapes...over and over again. Gondolas full of juicy grape bunches—still hand-picked, for the most part—make their way to wineries. Heady aromas of the "crush" pervade the air.

Finally, blends are essayed and assayed, possible aging regimes are evaluated, and wines are put to bed for the winter to begin the aging process. With time, they evolve into something more elegant, more complex than they ever were in their youth. Maturity, in wine, can be just as valued as that in humans.

world's wines

The "World" of Wine Out There

It is easy to think of wine as being restricted to the temperate zones of the third planet. Most of our "wine country" images are of Mediterranean "two season" climes (mild wet winter, warm dry summer): Tuscany, Bordeaux, Napa Valley, the River Duoro (Portugal), the Maipo Valley (Chile), Australia's Hunter Valley. Good grapes do not grow in ugly places.

But they can and do grow in "weather-ugly" places. Talk to the growers near the frigid 50th parallel along the Rheingau and Mosel in Germany, where they literally have to winch workers down those steep slate slopes. Talk to the growers in Canada's Niagara Peninsula, where "ice wine" is a dessert delicacy made from frozen grapes. Talk to my friends in Minnesota, where they have to dig a trench along their vine rows so as to *bury* their vines during their unremittingly frigid winters. Or home winegrowers in the south of England.

The key word of this tome is "variety." What we discover when we examine the world's wines is that they come from places beyond the easiest places for them to be grown—some great wines are made in garages!—and that they offer a range of flavors that are expansive almost beyond our ability to comprehend. The enduring fun of wine, I suggest to you, lies in our urge to examine that world, to expand our horizons, to taste, and be dazzled by the wondrous array that is available. There was a great poster at the San Francisco blood bank where I donated my first pint of the red. It was of a sailing ship under full sail. The caption: "A ship in a harbor is safe; but that's not what ships are built for." So taste, taste, and taste some more. Experience wine at its widest, at its most intriguing.

France:
"It Ain't Brag If You Can Do It"

Like it or no, what we know about quality wine starts with the French. Before Bordeaux, Burgundy, and Champagne insinuated themselves into our vinous consciousness, wine was no more than accidentally fermented grape juice. It was a commodity beverage and nothing more.

As recently as the late 1960s wine began to impress itself upon the American psyche, and we took our first models from the Gauls. (It's galling, I know.) At the outset, we learned about Cabernet Sauvignon from the *Bordelais*, we learned how to make Chardonnay from the Burgundians. Later, we took on Sauvignon Blanc and Pinot Noir, respectively, from the same two regions, adding as we went sparkling wine (Champagne), Chenin Blanc (the Loire), and Gewürztraminer (Alsace).

So put aside (mostly imagined) French *hauteur* and arrogance, and be grateful for their centuries of experience. The heritage they continue to pass down is what allows wine to expand its civilizing role in our society, bringing pleasure and culture to one and all.

The process is, fortunately, a continuing one. Ten years ago, few west of the Atlantic had any awareness of Rhône wines, and now we talk freely about Syrah, Grenache and Mourvedre, about Roussanne and Viognier. Malbec was little-known as a blending grape in Bordeaux until folks began talking about the wines of Cahors (in the southwest of France). The lighter reds of Burgundy—Beaujolais—were training-wheel wines for many of us, and we marked our true vinous sophistication when we came to understand the ineffable beauty of the succulent dessert wines of Sauternes and Barsac. The French may occasionally irritate but, as actor Walter Brennan reminded us in one of his crusty cowboy roles, "It ain't brag if you can do it."

Germany:
Cold Means "Racy"

The language of wine is odd. I remember the first time a German taster employed the term "racy" for a Riesling we were tasting. I flinched at the word, but when I tasted the wine I understood exactly what he meant. Germany's frigid climate produces white wines that literally "sing," their fruit is so pure and undiluted. There is such an incisive precision to the fruit and its underlying minerality, such a bell-tone clarity that "racy" is the only word that truly, clearly describes, indeed *informs* the phenomenon.

Germany's best are crisp, brightly-fruited whites like White Riesling and Mueller-Thurgau, which hail from the river regions of Rheingau and Mosel-Saar-Ruwer. These wines—which age remarkably well in bottle—make all manner of fish dishes, spicy Asian and Southwest cuisines, and picnic fare immeasurably better. Some red is produced from Pinot Noir (Spatburgunder) in Baden, and the sparkling wines are called *sekt*. (If you really understand your German sparkling wines, you are said to have passed *sekt* education.)

Sadly, many are put off by tightly-scripted, Gothic fonted, nearly indecipherable German wine labels that are, curiously, among the most informative in existence. They'll tell you the name of the producer, the region and vineyard the wine was grown in, and even the government's quality category, working upwards from *Tafelwein* (table wine), to QbA (district wine, in full *Qualitatsewein bestimmter Anbaugebiete*, and aren't you glad you asked?), to *Qualitatswein mit Pradikat* (quality wine from a specific location, QmP for short).

A word about the great dessert wines, usually from Riesling, sold under categories referring to the ripeness of the fruit at harvest: *Beerenauslese* (BAs) for "pretty darned sweet" and *trockenbeerenauslese* (TBAs) for "there's enough sugar here to remove the enamel from your teeth." Great with honeydew melon, or solo as dessert in a glass.

Italy:
Exuberance in a Bottle

If the French introduced us to distinctive wines of high quality, the Italians gave us leave to enjoy the fruit of the grape with an infectious energy and exuberance that changed the way we look at wine and food forever. For the Italians, wine is food and food is life. That's why in every hamlet and village, from Trentino to Trapani, you'll find local wines that seem to have been created solely for each site's cuisine.

The tangy Pinot Grigio of the Alto Adige, the floral white wines of Friuli, *Piemonte's* Barolo and Barbaresco (reds) and spicy-crisp Arneis (white), Tuscany's Chianti and Brunello di Montalcino (and the new Cabernet Sauvignon-based "Super Tuscans"), the sparkling wines of the north (*spumante*), the dried-berry dessert wines like *reciotto*, even the warm reds of Sicily: Each and every one reflects and enhances the exciting range of foodstuffs, from the basic pasta in red sauce to veal's delicacy, from shellfish to seafood, mushrooms to truffles…and those wonderful little crayfish they batter and fry that you toss in your mouth whole!

Italy is all about the senses, and the alluring confluence of smell, taste, and texture from both food and wine. I remember a luncheon *carpaccio* (raw beef, with olive oil and capers) in La Morra that was so devastatingly tasty that I would have ordered it again the next day…despite a wracking overnight case of food poisoning!

When you bring together the sweep of history, the range and beauty of geography, the hospitality of the people, the harmony of wine and food, there is no place on earth that comes close to Italy. Buy a cheap liter bottle of local wine at the grocer's, match it up with the locals' cuisine…and prepare to be dazzled. Exuberantly.

Portugal:
Green, Pink, and Red...and Port

Despite the charming scaled-back ambition of her people, Portugal has some strong underpinnings of pride when it comes to wine. While many of her wines are resolutely rustic, produced solely for local consumption—the spritzy "green" wines (*vinho verde*) and the coarse reds—a solid part of Portugal's vinous reputation is based on two wines created for export: The wildly popular rosés (Mateus and Lancer's originally) and the enduringly praised wines bottled at the Duoro River's terminus at Oporto: Port.

While the rosés are simple, easy "picnic" wines, *vinho verdes* are crisp, fizzy white wines that are ideal with the country's famous *caldo verde* soup (potato, chorizo sausage, and greens). That combination can take me back to my Portuguese grandmother's kitchen in the time it takes their fragrances to reach my nose.

Port—and its island relative, Madeira—are known everywhere. Grapes grown on sun-drenched slopes are blended with high-proof brandy to create dessert wines that can stand on their own, or match up to a wide array of postprandial creations, from cheddar cheese to fruit tarts, Portugal's *arroz doce* (rice pudding) or flan (a delicate caramelized dessert made with Port). The best Ports—Graham, Dow, Quinta do Noval, Cockburn—possess a silky richness, where the alcohol is mere sidelight it is so artfully integrated into the wine. They are capable of great age. (Curiously, even the White Ports eventually end up the same tawny brown color as those produced from red grape varieties.)

Portuguese table wines are improving dramatically, especially reds from the Douro (home of Port) and from the more southern regions of Dão and Bairrada (known for tender suckling pig, which goes great with the reds). Keep an open mind...and a questioning nose.

Spain:
Sherry and Sparklers, and More

Like Portugal, much of what we know of this Iberian Peninsula country's wines has to do with dessert: In this case, Sherry. Yet, here too, there are other wines to stretch our experience, broaden our vinous horizons.

Even the old tried-and-true Sherry comes in a wide range of styles, from the delicate, almond-scented, ethereal *finos*—which are dry and rather low in alcohol and best served chilled—to the increasingly sweet wines grown on Spain's southwestern frontier at Jerez ("hair-ETH"): *palo cortado, amontillado, oloroso,* cream. You probably know many of the prime producers by name: Domecq, Lustau, Sandeman, Gonzalez Byass, Harvey's.

The region of Cataluña (southeastern Spain, radiating out of the exquisite port city of Barcelona)—which even has its own language, the people are so independent—is known for exquisitely inexpensive sparkling wines, locally called *cavas*, particularly from Codorniu, Freixenet, and Torres. There are also distinctive table wines from Cataluña (the overall wine region is called Penedès), some made from French varieties like Cabernet, others Rhône-like in the rapidly rising sub-region of Priorato, southwest of Barcelona.

We're also learning more recently of the northern regions, where red wines of note are grown in the Rioja, Ribera del Duero, and Navarra and produced by companies like Cune, Vega Sicilia, and Pesquera. Pay particular attention to reds labeled *Riserva* and *Gran Riserva*, which have had longer time in wood and bottle, and are thus soft and ready to drink at point of purchase. The adventurous spirit is always the most rewarded, so taste and discover for yourself, and learn the proper use of that most endearing and Hemingway-esque of Spanish words, olé!

California:
Heaven on Earth

Wine first came to California with the Spanish padres, extending their Franciscan faith up the *El Camino Real* ("Royal Road"), the chain of missions built in Mexico and California. The fiery, fierce wines and brandies the padres produced were made ostensibly for the Mass.

Winegrowing's infancy as a business came as an offshoot of the 1849 Gold Rush, hung on as a cottage industry through pest and prohibition—each farmer growing grapes for home wine—until the 1970s, when serious consumers pushed hobby into vocation.

California is special because the Golden State has a gamut of climes that is unparalleled in the universe we know. There are the chilly coastal reaches—Anderson Valley, Russian River Valley, Santa Ynez Valley—where Pinot Noir and Chardonnay shine, both for silky table wines and crisp sparkling wines. Gewürztraminer shimmers in coastal "cool."

As you move inland, you explore Sonoma County and Napa Valley in the north, and the vast north-south range of the Central Coast (San Francisco to Santa Barbara), for varieties as varied as Cabernet Sauvignon, Merlot, Syrah, Chardonnay, and Sauvignon Blanc.

Then there's the great inland plain—the San Joaquin and Sacramento valleys—where Chenin Blanc and Zinfandel create table wines expensive in taste at a price pleasing to the pocketbook, along with a wondrous array of dessert wines, from low alcohol Muscats to Port-styled wines rich with plum and walnut essences. In the Sierra Foothills—what was once Gold Country—dozens of cottage wineries craft exciting wines from Zinfandel, Syrah, and Barbera varieties.

Nearly 90 percent of American wines are grown in California, where producers range from the world's largest to tiny garage and industrial park bays, where serious folk tend to their art with mind and heart conjoined. The results are, in a word, breathtaking.

Napa Valley and Sonoma County:
"Sonapanoma"

It is a given that, like it or not, appellations influence both the price of grapes and how we buy wines. "Napa" and "Sonoma" are the pearls of California's premium appellations and image. That they are occasionally confused can be a sore point—as when Jordan or Chateau St. Jean are identified as "Napa Valley" wineries—but grapes grown in these two places have a cachet that is unmatched in the United States. (A 2003 survey showed that a bottle of "Napa Valley" wine, all other things being equal, cost $20 more than a bottle labeled with "California.")

Napa is most known because its crescent-shaped valley is so utterly devoted to the grape. State Highway 29, running parallel to the Napa River, is called "The Wine Road," and more than 250 wineries populate the county between the Carneros (along the coast of San Francisco's Bay) and the markedly warmer Calistoga to the north. Cabernet Sauvignon is clearly king in the warmer mid- and upper-valley locations—Rutherford and Stags Leap— and particularly on its view-inspiring hillside slopes. Chardonnay, Pinot Noir, and Merlot come into focus in the fog-cooled Carneros.

Closer to the Pacific Coast, Sonoma County has a smorgasbord variety of appellations, from its own Carneros, Sonoma Coast and Russian River "cool" to the Cabernet and Zinfandel "warm" of Sonoma, Alexander, Knights and Dry Creek valleys. Large numbers of *fin de siecle* Italian settlers found places that reminded them of Piedmont and Tuscany, creating hearty red wines full of flavor. Explore beyond the usual suspects—Cabernet, Chardonnay, Pinot Noir, Merlot—and search out "fun" wines like Sauvignon Blanc, Gewürztraminer, Zinfandel, Barbera, Syrah, Sangiovese. Sonoma is as diverse as any place on the planet, and as such it is just the place for the most adventuresome amongst us.

Oregon and Washington:
Hot and Cold, Sort of

Seemingly linked by their Pacific Northwest "coastal" locations, Oregon and Washington are actually quite unalike. Because most of Oregon's vine zones nearly abut the Pacific, Oregon is, in winespeak, "cold," while most of Washington's viniculture is east of the Cascade mountain range: "warm."

That's why you start with cold climate varieties in Oregon: Pinot Noir (spicy black cherry), Chardonnay (green apple), Pinot Gris (a mineral-crisp white that's coming on strong of late), Gewürztraminer (alive with floral spiciness), and White Riesling (with its racy stone-like qualities). These are wines that retain sufficient acidity to "frame" fruit artfully and decisively. David Lett (The Eyrie Vineyard) pioneered the Willamette Valley (Yamhill County, just southwest of Portland) in 1966. This is Oregon's heartland, and some of the world's most velvety, most sensual Pinot Noirs call this verdant valley home. Further south, particularly in the Rogue River Valley, it is actually warm enough to mature Cabernet Sauvignon grapes. Also, try on Oregon's zesty fruit and berry wines for size, particularly the boysenberry and blackberry. (We learned just how hot "cool" Oregon was when the 1980s brought vinous investors from France, California, and Australia.)

Second only to California in wine production (having passed New York), Washington is, in terms of climate, something of "Bordeaux West": Merlot shines softly with black currant fruit, Cabernet Sauvignon is blackberry precise, and Cabernet Franc, Malbec, and Petit Verdot are often used in red "Bordeaux" blends; on the white side, Sauvignon Blanc and Semillon are extraordinarily expressive, especially when blended together. Chateau Ste. Michelle (and linked label Columbia Crest) are reliable Merlot producers, Hogue and Columbia do Sauvignon Blanc/Semillon justice, and Leonetti is a red wine highlight film. New to apple country are dazzling Syrahs and Sangioveses.

The Rest of the U.S.:
Working Outward from The "Big Apple"

The greatest boon to an adventurous spirit—even for the most beginning of wine aficionados—is the fact that every one of the 50 states now has at least one winery. And very nearly all have a vineyard or two. Which means that any American can find a winery close to home and discover, first hand, that wine is nothing more mysterious than carefully tended grape juice that gets added life and extra interest from its modest alcohol content.

If New York City is the "Big Apple," there are no wineries on Manhattan. But from Long Island (Bordeaux varieties shine), through the verdant Hudson River Valley and on up into the autumnal beauty of the Finger Lakes (crisp, steely Mosel-like Rieslings), New York is wine country.

So is the rest of the country. I remember hosting a fascinating, sold-out dinner in which regional cuisines were paired with wines from the regions: A tangy sparkling wine from Hawaii with the *hors d'oeuvres*, Smithfield ham with lemon-rich Chardonnays from Maryland and Ohio, a rabbit ragout with the Pinot Noir-like Leon Millot (Minnesota) and pepper-spiced Norton (Missouri), Charolais prime rib with Arkansas and Maryland Cabernets, and assorted cheeses with a crisp Arkansas Riesling.

Explore your palate as you explore your own backyard and discover wines like Seyval Blanc or Vignoles and the vinous identities of Wisconsin, Michigan, Texas, the Four Corners, Georgia. All those places have serious folk devoting serious time and money to the cultivation of the grape toward its most noble form: wine. There is a veritable cornucopia of types and styles to choose from, a plethora of artistic expression that is sure to raise a smile and a nod, from novice to expert. What could be more fun?

Australia and New Zealand:
Kangaroos to Kiwis

"Down Under" conjures up a variety of images, from kiwi (fruit and bird) to marsupial, from grass-court tennis to great helicopter skiing. And wines of extraordinary flavor intensity and terrific pocketbook value from locales like McLaren Vale, Yarra Valley, Coonawarra, Barossa Valley, Hunter River.

The saucy Aussies initially made their vinous mark abroad with succulent, wood-aged Semillons dubbed, with their casual irreverence, "Hunter Riesling." Then there was the classic Grange Hermitage, a full-bodied red wine made from Shiraz that vaulted Australia into international prominence. (I remember tasting the wine with the late Max Schubert, then Penfolds' winemaker, when a dozen Italian winemakers joined in. They were dazzled by the wine's length, heft, and size. Said one, "In Italy, we could make *six* wines from this!")

The New Zealanders came to our attention a bit more than a decade ago with Sauvignon Blancs that were almost intended to *be the meal*, what with all that fresh and undiluted fruit openly hanging out for all to see. Now we see their devotion to cooler locations (Otago, Gisbourne, Wellington, Martinborough, Nelson) with Pinot Noirs supple and sensual in texture and markedly clear in their fruit exposition. Chardonnay is also grown, along with Cabernet and Merlot, in the warmer locations (Marlborough, Hawkes Bay).

New Zealand appeals to the optimist in us. It is a smallish country—about the size of Colorado—and its vinelands are about two-thirds that of Sonoma County. But it offers myriad opportunities, from the depth and beauty of its Maori cultural history to the vast range of recreational landscapes (from surf to snow in the bat of an eyelash). Their vinous range is nearly as great, with wines boasting brittle acidity that makes them ideal with spicy or fusion cuisine. Something for everyone, for sure.

Chile and Argentina:
Farmers and Cowboys

As to Chile, lock on to the fact that their fruit growers have long been the world's most fastidious. I recall visiting a winery that produced excellent wines despite the fact that their winemaking facility was weak-walled, dirt-floored, and had wooden barrels older than granny. Their secret? The best fruit going. (That winery is now owned by the Rothschilds, and its facility now matches its fruit.)

Indeed, California, French, and Spanish money is now awash in Chile, and wineries are able to handle quality fruit in ways they never could before, resulting in fruit-friendly wines at ridiculously reasonable prices. Carmenère, a red Bordeaux variety, makes a tobacco-rich red that is utterly charming, and the Merlots (blackberry) and Cabernet Sauvignons (cassis and coffee) are equally alluring. The Maipo and Colchagua valleys are well known for quality, and Casablanca, closer to the Pacific, is an up-and-coming appellation to keep an eye on.

As to Argentina, wine is gaucho-driven: Brusque reds to match up to their best beef. There is a tango of change afoot, as growers seek out cooler locations to create wines of greater finesse and complexity. Even those in the main Mendoza Valley—in the eastern foothills of the Andes and nearly the size of California's entire wine industry—are moving skyward in altitude to find cooler pockets (up to nearly 6000 feet above sea level!). The Mendoza Valley accounts for three of every four bottles produced in Argentina.

Darkly-colored, tannin-sharp Malbec may be the most identifiable quality wine grown today in the land of Evita, often showing intense black currant, coffee, espresso, and chocolate notes that do, certainly, invite the medium-rare prime rib or its ilk. Cabernet Sauvignon (cassis and bittersweet chocolate) and Chardonnay (tropical pear and pineapple fruit) are also grown extensively in this region.

Memoir:
Traveling the World's Beauteous Wine Regions

The simple fact of the matter is this: Great wines do not grow in ugly places. Sure, there are broad plains where table grapes and grapes for ordinary wines grow along with the corn. But those rare locales where terrain and *terroir* come together perfectly—sparse, loose soils, the right sun exposure, the proximity to a large, cooling water mass—inevitably have a stark and spare beauty about them that is beguiling.

I am half Portuguese, and vividly remember my first trip up the Duoro River, home of the world's signature Ports. The steep hillsides are terraced with rock walls put together with a craftsmanship almost mystical in its precision. The terraces seem ancient fortresses, with elfin vines guarding their precious fruit like tiny soldiers.

Along the River Loire in France, the fortresses are real stone chateaux that conjure up images of knights in armor agleam, the vineyards more feminine, the landscape softer. Italy's *Piemonte* has a similar feminine gracefulness in its green, undulating hills, while Tuscany, to the south, is a brown, sere, rocky, masculine presence. Does it seem to you, too, that the Tuscan wines are also more severe, a bit harder than the Barolos and Barbarescos of *Piemonte*? In the north, in the apple country of the Alto Adige, are starkly beautiful hillsides where Pinot Noir and Pinot Gris have been grown for centuries. There, one family has been in the wine business since the late 1700s, and their oldest cellar pre-dates Christopher Columbus!

My German half utterly thrills to the river boat ride along the Rhein (or Mosel). The steep slate slopes are daunting, so shear they literally have to lower vineyard workers on winch cable lines so they can tend their highly productive vines. (The Germans are the most efficient grape growers in the world, coaxing high yields in conjunction with amazing quality, each perfect vine producing at peak capability.)

To the east is Alsace, once German, now French. In the historic town of Riquewihr (near Strasbourg), some 90 percent of the houses date from before 1600! There, weekend wine fairs are festive, fueled as they are by the apple-crisp Pinot Gris wines of the region.

The wine valleys of Chile are framed by their dramatic proximity to the Andes. Fanning out north and south from Santiago, they stand in the shadow of snow-capped mountain peaks that feel as close as your elbow, so sharply do they rise up to meet the horizon. There is an ancient feel to the vineyards here, as there are few mechanized vehicles once you leave the city, and you see most people afoot and riding two-to-a-bicycle.

The land is much flatter on the oldest continent, Australia, where most of its wine valleys are braced by low rolling hills that meander aimlessly. Which is typical of the Aussie's sassy, easy irreverence. Who else would refer to honied dessert wines as "stickies?"

Though we have a much younger wine industry, there are plenty of splendid American vineland destinations. Vines face Lake Erie in Ohio, in Minnesota they are literally buried to withstand freezing winters, and I remember fondly going frog-gigging in Missouri with a winemaker who assured me that frog legs were great with Seyval Blanc. (He was right.) The Finger Lakes (New York), the Columbia Valley (Washington and Oregon), the Napa Valley (California) are sights to behold.

One place I yearn to see is South Africa, where vines are shadowed by shear mountain formations, the likes of which I have only seen thus far in photographs. At least I've tasted their wines, which only serve to make the wish to be there that much more fervent.

Wine and Your Health:
It Works for Most of Us

One thing must be eminently clear from the outset in this discussion: Wine isn't for everyone. Fully 10 percent of most adult populations physiologically cannot metabolize alcohol, and thus ought not consume wine.

Let's start with the liabilities of alcohol, because they do exist: U.S. health care costs attributed to alcohol are staggering, perhaps $150 billion a year; the fact is, some alcoholic beverages are marketed to teens as if they were as harmless as soda pop.

Unfortunately, Americans tend to approach alcohol the same way they approach sex. In reaction to repressive teachings, many of us handle both with little in the way of knowledge or responsibility as we battle our way past puberty. The problem with repressive teaching techniques is that they inordinately skew perspective. The forbidden fruit—be it alcohol or sex—takes on an importance out of all reasonable proportion. That's why youngsters often think of sex as love, alcohol as "adult."

The answer, in both cases, is education and (excuse the word) exposure. In other cultures, where wine is routinely served to youngsters—in dilute form—those children understand early on that there is a responsible manner in which wine may be used. In other cultures, where there is no Puritanical taboo on sex, the subject is openly discussed so that when the hormones start pumping, it comes as no sudden surprise to these kids.

This is not to say that wine, no matter its many valuable attributes, should be lionized or romanticized. Yes, wine sharpens appetite, aids in digestion, and elevates conversation—but only when used with great awareness.

Alcohol, like any other drug, has both beneficial dosage and toxic dosage. For those who lack the enzyme needed to usefully metabolize alcohol, any consumption, in any form, at any time is toxic.

For most of us, though, the dosage is the key. Unlike cigarettes—where any level of use is toxic—alcohol is a double-edged sword: On one side there is positive benefit; on the other, there is danger and damage. There was an article in *Scientific American* quite some time ago whose thesis was that alcohol, had it not been previously discovered, would now, upon its discovery, be hailed as drug more valuable in its widespread use than penicillin. The author supported his case by citing the natural tranquilizing effect of wine, especially for hospital and nursing home patients for whom a glass of wine at mealtime and/or bedtime improves digestion and induces restful sleep that might otherwise elude them.

This is not to mention the vast and increasingly impressive body of evidence that a glass or two of wine with the evening meal reduces circulatory and cardiac risk by up to 50 percent. That's a healthy reduction in heart problems, our number one killer. Of equal interest, the proofs demonstrate that it's better to drink moderately than not at all.

This is what we know for sure: Alcohol, like an automobile or any other potentially destructive tool, has its beneficial level of use and its deleterious level of use. For that reason, one must take the arguments of wine's most ardent proponents *and* those of the neo-prohibitionist terrorists with the proverbial grain of salt. In both cases, their words are defending overtly and overly sacred territory.

Listen rather, I submit, to those moderate voices that preach caution and awareness. Even some beer producers are aware enough to use popular pooches and professional athletes to counsel kids to "know when to say when." That's sound advice, be it about alcohol or sex.

wine country

One Person's Passion is Another Man's Poison

This is the entire theme of this book. The Romans, with their lust for the good life, said it thusly: *"De gustibus non est disputandum,"* (In matters of taste, there are no disputes).

It was when I began to work as a wine judge, here and abroad, that I quickly began to comprehend this truism's fullest import. There I was, judging wines with winemakers, retailers and writers with international reputations . . . and there were wines that some loved and others utterly hated! How did we come to such total disagreement?

People have different tastes. It's as simple as that. Whenever I was on a panel with the late writer Jerry Mead, I knew for certain that at some point he would wander over with a glass of red. I knew that the wine would be loaded with *brettanomyces.* "Brett," in small amounts, offers a touch of complexity to a red wine, with its characteristic leather or fish oil smell. It is often found in French Burgundies. But when brett begins to dominate, it shows off its essential nature. It's a spoilage bacteria. Let's review: A little, for those who like it, adds complexity; a lot, especially for those who don't like it, renders the wine undrinkable. Jerry really liked brett; I tolerate, even enjoy it at low levels.

One other example. I was in Italy, sitting on a panel with four Italian winemakers, who wanted to award high marks to a severely spoiled wine. Through an interpreter I asked why they would honor a wine that was so obviously flawed? "To encourage the winemaker," they replied. To do what, I wondered? Keep making bad wine?

Our mantra is this: Your palate is the one that counts. Drink what *you* like.

Need a Cellar Book?

The short answer, No. Absolutely not. Waste of paper, waste of time, and a waste of energy.

The long answer, Maybe. The great thing about keeping a record of the wines you collect, and your tasting notes, is that you have a permanent image of how your palate has evolved.

When I first began to seriously annotate my wine tasting, my cellar was devoted to Cabernet Sauvignon and Chardonnay. Those were the wines that "serious" imbibers imbibed in the early 1970s. What is clear to see, as I look back over my notes, is that I gradually began to shift my attentions toward Pinot Noir and Sauvignon Blanc. Nothing consistent about that, actually, going from lean to opulent on the red side, and the opposite direction with regard to white wines. But that was what my palate was telling me I liked.

A cellar book also allows you to follow a given wine over the years, that 1968 Beaulieu Private Reserve Cabernet just got better over two decades, with its black currant and green olive fruit softening and growing more complex, or the 1981 Chateau Lynch Bages that got deeper with its cassis and menthol fruit. The wonderful surprise of the "lost" case of 1984 Trefethen Chardonnay that turned out to be wonderfully silky and succulent when we found it after a decade hidden in a dusty corner. And a bottle of 40-year-old German sparkling wine to celebrate the birth of our twins in 1987.

It's amusing to just leaf through and find notes to yourself. On apricot wine: "Drink it young!" On Navarro's Cluster Select Late Harvest Riesling: "Honey and apricot of such depth and duration." The references to exotic wines from Minnesota and Ohio, to former "exotics" from Chile and New Zealand and South Africa. It's all there in the cellar book, your wine diary, your wine history. A record of your very own palate.

How to Read a Label

German labels are the most confusing, with all that information and the unreadable Gothic font, but American wine labels aren't that much better.

All the information you really need from a label is the producer, the wine type, the vintage date, and region/vineyard in which the grapes were grown. The rest is often more than we need to know. (To be fair, it can be helpful to know the alcohol content when there is a difference between a delicate Riesling at seven percent and a hefty dessert wine at 22 percent. But do we really need to know if the wine was "unfiltered" or "unfined" or "aged in Nevers oak"?)

It helps to know that, for American wines, varietal wines (those named for the primary grape variety, as Chardonnay or Zinfandel) are required to have at least 75 percent of the named grape. Does that mean that a red wine with only 50 percent Cabernet Sauvignon is an inferior wine to one with 75 percent (or 100

percent)? Depends on what the other half is, and where the fruit was grown. Some of the best red wines in the world are blends of two to five of the Bordeaux varieties (often sold under a proprietary name or the stylistic name "Meritage").

It also helps to know that where American wines list a specific appellation, at least 85 percent of the grapes must come from the named locale. For vintage-dated wines, at least 95 percent of the wine must be from that harvest.

As we have discussed, the most reliably useful word on any label is identity of the producer. The producer's name will tell you more than any other words on the label about the quality, style, and consistency of the wine inside. Keep that in mind, and you'll rarely be disappointed.

Visiting Wine Country

Wine is a social beverage, and nowhere do you see that aspect more than when visiting wine country. Many wineries now offer picnic facilities, some even have deli items to fill out your picnic larder. More and more offer their facilities for social gatherings, from weddings to corporate meetings and special dinners.

Just keep your wits about you when touring wine country. Rule number one is this: Stay sober. If you are visiting more than one winery in a day, learn to spit after tasting. Swallow, and you'll be a candidate for a DUI ticket at best, vehicular manslaughter at worst. I have tasted more than a hundred wines a day judging at wine competitions worldwide without absorbing more than trace amounts of alcohol . . . by conscientiously spitting out each sample. Find the spit bucket and save a life (or two).

Beyond that, the rules of common courtesy apply. Be polite. Be neat. Respect those who work at the winery and those who are visiting. Lounging and lunching casually at a winery picnic table is a terrific moment to meditate on the bounty of the earth and how the earth expresses its personality, its "place-ness" through the food it provides, the distinctive wines it proffers, the gorgeous vistas it presents.

In true wine country—Napa Valley, Bordeaux—you might be able to visit a half dozen wineries in a day (though that's stretching it a bit, in my book). My favorite touring day was in Texas some years back. Starting in Dallas, a Beechcraft *King Air* took us to Lubbock to visit Llano Estacado Winery, then to the Hill Country to visit the Aulers at Fall Creek, followed by a Jeep ride over to Crystal Valley. (I got to fly the *King Air* part of the way.) What a day!

Humor:
Strange and Crummy Wineries I Have Visited

The increasing wonder of technology aside, winery visits are not always picnics and Chardonnay. There remain wineries strange and wineries downright crummy out there. This category is an odd lot, a quaint, small, and dying grouping.

Easily the worst winery in which I've ever set foot once held sway in the Arkansas foothills near Altus, cheek-by-jowl with a couple of surprisingly good ones (Post and Wiederkehr). This place was a disaster waiting to happen, and perhaps it did. The last time I was there the wooden structure looked as if it would fall to the next decent northern blow, the boards were so lazily attached to their cross beams.

Inside, the winery was no better. Much of the floor was dirt, and barrels and tanks seemed to have rated no better attention than the building itself. I assumed that sanitation was not a word known to the proprietor. Indeed, this winery had been the butt of the finest bad-wine story I have ever heard, a story—whose teller, an Episcopal priest, swears by all that is good and just—that is wholly and completely true. In short, the winemaker sent one of his white wines to the Arkansas State Laboratory for analysis. The report came back (the priest swears this is true!): "Your horse has diabetes!"

That is the most lacerating put-down of a wine I have heard in my 30-plus years in wine. Far superior to the "100-year-old, dirty sweat socks" description of a Mongolian Mare's Milk wine I tasted a couple of decades ago, or the familiar "cat piss" occasionally ascribed to Sauvignon Blanc (as a positive, no less). No, I cannot ever think of the "horse" line without busting a gut laughing, it is such a tonic for depression. (Speaking of horses, we once started a "horse wine" game during winter doldrums when I was working at a winery tasting room early in my career. Came up with Pinto Noir, the old grey Merlot, Foal Blanche, Appaloosa *Controlee*, and the like.)

There was once a cave winery hidden in the folds of the Santa Cruz Mountains that was pretty grungy. The barrels were a bit better cared for than those of our Arkansas friend, but there was enough mold hanging from the bare dirt-and-rock walls to create one of the all-time great Halloween horror houses. Their wine quality was always a crap shoot.

There was another one, north of San Diego. I'm sure the fellow's audience was older Italian men who didn't mind a lot of volatile acidity because his Zinfandel was fairly riddled with the stuff. So much so, that I could smell the vinegar clearly from the shot glass he poured the wine into…four feet away! A row of cork-finished bottles displayed behind the tasting counter had fill levels that undulated like a roller-coaster ride in profile.

I also recall a couple of crummy wineries that actually made terrific wines under the most dire of circumstances. Take the old San Martin Winery as prime example. The wines were great. That was a testament to San Martin's late winemaker, Ed Friedrich, one of California's finest winemakers. It was Ed who, at San Martin in the 1970s, gave us the inimitable treat of "soft" wines, like his nine percent alcohol Johannisberg Riesling, a wine of such freshness and vitality that our understanding of what California wines could be changed at that very moment, immediately and forever.

San Martin, before an infusion of capital by a new owner spiffed up the place, was a collection of ancient equipment in an outdated and crumbling old building. Both facility and equipment looked, at first glance, filthy. But closer inspection would detect a rigorous regime of sanitation, because Friedrich was German-born and relentless in his pursuit of quality. Ed had the knack for searching out excellent grapes, and would brook no bounds to keep their juice away from impurities. He was so good, that he later produced outstanding wines in both Arkansas (there again!) and Georgia before his untimely passing from cancer in 1986.

Another was the old Los Vascos, in Chile, before the Rothschild franc infusion. Their old cellar could have cultured some pretty interesting organisms, critters that would have made any biologist worth his or her salt stand up and take notice (and, perhaps, come up with the cure for some off-beat disease in the meanwhile). The cooperage was old and shaggy, and sanitation was miss more than hit. But their vineyards produced stunningly definitive fruit that the wines overcame their cellar surroundings.

Now days, it's pretty hard to find truly crummy (read "unsanitary") wineries, because in the super-competitive climate of today they simply couldn't last beyond a vintage or two. Indeed, one former crummy winery in the North Coast—where two feet of red wine lees were once found to be the culprit in a tank of "red-tinged" Chardonnay—has since had a complete makeover and is routinely turning out wines of distinction and elegance.

So now we'll just have to settle for the occasional oddball and his or her "strange" ways and strange winery. Let me know when you spot one, so I can add to my private listing. God and Goddess forbid we should be restricted to visiting hospital-clean production plants with all the personality of poorly programmed robots.

How to Spot "Rotten" Grapes

No artistic device delivers more impact than that of the "devil-turns-out-to-be-hero." Don Diego de la Vega, cowardly fop by day, nightly dons his black cape to carve Z's on the bad guys. An ordinary mold, fit only to be rubbed away by a washcloth turns out to be penicillin. Huzzah! Hurray!

Botrytis is a blue-gray mold that forms on grape berries in periods of alternating humidity and heat during harvest. This "noble rot" does not wear a black cape, nor does it carry quite the healing impact of penicillin. But the salubrious effects of botrytis on grape juice has been known to chase the blues, and that ain't bad, bub.

Botrytis was once held in disdain, along with a wide variety of other molds, until it was discovered to have properties more than beneficial a couple of centuries ago in Germany. This by way of Schloss Johannisberg where, in 1775, the harvest courier returned late with the permission of the Prince-Abbot of Fulda to commence the harvest—by which time the overripe grapes were shriveled with rot. But the wine was made anyway. The French claim, by way of Chateau d'Yquem, is similar on all accounts, but doesn't happen until 1847, according to Count Alexandre de Lur-Saluces.

Here's what actually happens. The mold causes the grapes to dehydrate, but the skins remain intact. That vastly increases the concentration of sugar and acid, and the mold adds a "honey-like" character to the resulting wines, which are thick and syrup sweet. Yields are reduced dramatically, but flavors are magically intensified.

The wines are, in short, among the most revered in the world, being rich, succulent, and sweet. Rieslings, German and American, can approach apricot syrup in consistency and taste, while French Sauternes (Semillon and Sauvignon Blanc blends) flash a phantasm of fruit flavors, including honey, peaches, bananas, figs, and goodness knows what else. It's enough to breathlessly say "Wow!" and just wallow in the pleasure of it all.

The Aussies have the best nickname for the genre. They call them "stickies," the wines are so sweet, so syrupy. Note that rarely is the word "botrytis" used on the label to mark these wines. In this country, they're usually referred to as "Late Harvest" wines. Which is funny, because grapes infected with botrytis are often picked *earlier* than non-mold-infected fruit.

Botrytised wines first came to California in the late 1950s, when Myron and Alice Nightingale began experimenting by inoculating normally ripe grapes with the mold in the lab at the old Cresta Blanca Winery (Livermore). Nearby, at Wente Brothers, Karl Wente began making a botrytised Riesling from their Monterey fruit in 1969, and in 1973 Freemark Abbey made their first "Edelwein" from Riesling. Soon Chateau St. Jean, Joseph Phelps, Beringer, Firestone, and Navarro were producing superb Rieslings, and the occasional Late Harvest Gewürztraminer. Far Niente's Dolce is California's finest Sauternes equivalent.

Whether you prefer traditional French Sauternes and Barsaces, the German beauties, or the wonderful California treats, these are among the most exquisite dessert wines made on the third planet. Served with the complement of fruit, the contrast of blue cheese, or simply by their own sweet selves, these wines typify the theatrical twist by turning a malevolent mold into syrupy, sensual sweetness. And that's worth a Huzzah! Or two.

There is an additional advantage to these wines: If you ever suspect that someone is not from the third planet, all you have to do to confirm your suspicions is to offer them a glass of one of these wines. If they do not take to it avidly, they must certainly be an alien!

The Grape Grower:
Character Impersonated

As you sip a glass wine, consider the *essence* of what's in that glass. All of the romance, all of the flavor came from a foundation—in the best sense of that word—of farming.

Growers are the best people in all of wine. There's no salesman slick, there's none of the artistic posturing associated with winemakers. Farmers are simply people who work straight, walk straight, and talk straight. For the farmer, something either works or it doesn't. It's a refreshing approach.

It is a perspective, I think, born of having to battle Ma Nature on even terms throughout the year, knowing full well that perfection of effort will not necessarily earn success comes harvest. Knowing that a year's worth of effort can be destroyed by drought or storm—sometimes in a single day—brings humility, farsightedness, and perspective, most attractive qualities.

A Sonoma winery once had a second label that framed an Honoré Daumier lithograph of a grape grower and his assistant inspecting their vines. The assistant has a brace of wooden grape stakes over his shoulder and the ancient, withered grower is hunched closely over a vine, saying, "We have just escaped the frost. Now all we have to fear is the heat, the rain, the grape disease, and all the rest!" It must be several times funnier to those of us who do not grow grapes for a living.

Better still is the attitude of competing *with* rather than *against* one another. In what other industry do you have a Robert Mondavi, who not only does not fire employees starting their own wineries, but encourages them with advice, training, and bargains on used equipment?! It starts with the growers, a fiercely independent lot, who nonetheless find time and energy to support one another just as fiercely. It's pride, humanity, and character.

Wine Scams:
What to Believe?

With all the vinous verbiage spewed out of computers during the last few decades—not to mention sharp improvements in wine quality, worldwide—you'd think that American wine consumption would have tripled in that time. It has not. Indeed, if per capita adult wine consumption in the U.S. were graphed, and placed on a chart at the foot of a patient's bed…the doc would assume "dead critter." Flat line.

Though wine consumption is down a bit in Europe, the French and Italians continue to consume six times what we do, and even the beer-loving Aussies double our consumption. Why is that, do you suppose?

How about the arrogant, elitist, separatist manner that all too many folks in the wine business perpetuate? For some reason, vintners here cling to what I call the "candlelight and caviar" syndrome, a mode that had sold every bottle it could ever sell three decades ago! That is why fewer than 10 percent of Americans serve wine on a regular basis, and it's not getting any better.

The wine scams of the Western world also contribute to this lethargy among consumers. This is (mis)information so "in" that it turns most folks off to wine before they even get a chance to trust their own palate.

The "Reserve" Scam: "Reserve" wines are always better than a winery's regular wine. Uh huh. And "New and Improved" is always about quality and never about price. Believe these, and I'm back in the bridge business. First off, even presuming that a winery *intends* to create a better wine with its Reserve offering—and I don't doubt their intent—all too often these are merely wines that are overmade—overripe fruit, extra "new" oak aging, higher alcohol, more fruit extract—to the point of becoming caricatures of the winery's better balanced, better drinking "regular" wines.

The Wine Judging Scam: The wine community, for its own selfish, controlling reasons perpetuates the myth that someone else (worse still, some consensus opinion) can tell you what wines you should like. And, for some truly unknown reason, many consumers buy into this ridiculous notion. I have never understood why the same person who would never allow someone else to dictate his or her taste in art, music, food, automobiles, or literature...turns around and asks, "What wine should I like?"

The whole system takes on yet more ludicrous form when wine scores are divvied up on a 100-point scale. How, exactly, does a wine scored 93 differ from one scored 92? Anyone who has ever watched a wine competition panel work—it's similar to the joke about watching sausage being made or laws being enacted—knows that widely acknowledged "experts" can totally disagree on individual wines. You know the rule here: In matters of taste, trust your own instincts. You know what you like better than anyone else on the planet.

The Appellation Scam: We've already discussed this one. Though where a wine comes from does offer some qualitative information—we know that Pinot Noir is certainly going to be better from the Russian River Valley than from any warmer inland valley—if you want *quality* information from the label it has to come from a producer's name and reputation.

The Restaurant Wine Price Scam: Restaurateurs love to say that they have to put wine glasses out, store the wines, and even open the bottle (that's heavy lifting!)—all in justification for bottle prices so exorbitant that I have seen a glass of wine priced *higher than the retail price of the bottle it came from!* Sorry gang, but you've got to put out linen, silverware, and even bring the plates to the table, too. Restaurant wine prices do not have to mimic spirits prices. Restaurant owners who scale back their wine prices quickly discover that more people buy wine, the wine enhances the taste of the food and the extent of diners' conversational abilities, and

they tell their friends. Wouldn't you think that those elements would improve a restaurant's popularity (and profitability)? Me, too.

The Candlelight and Caviar Syndrome: I was once corralled by a wealthy winery owner castigating wine writers for not bringing more Americans to wine. Not ready to fight, I declined to point out that she traveled First Class, showed her wines only at top hotels, and thus had a rather myopic view of where the marketplace for wine is these days.

That's the problem with ivory-tower thinking. We'd rather stay above the fray, and consequently out of touch with the many valid reasons that most Americans pass on our beloved "improved grape juice." If it were up to me, I'd be closing all but top-of-the-line chateau stuff with screw caps or crown caps, or employing bag-in-box convenience. And I'd teach people to say *Gewürztraminer* when someone sneezes. If we can learn to say *gesundheit* we can certainly learn to pronounce *Gewürztraminer*, don't you think?

Consider where that could lead. We learn to pronounce *Gewürztraminer*. We begin to order it with confidence. We discover the charming nature of this enchanting wine. We try other wines, discover that we like some, dislike others . . . and will consume some if someone else foots the bill.

In short we develop confidence enough to know what we like. Learn to say *Gewürztraminer*, or even just *Gewürz*, and you become a wine lover.

The Restaurant:
Wine Cathedral or Wine Dungeon?

Speaking of restaurants, they ought to be the best places to consume wine. Eating out is often an occasion, a festivity amplified by the presence of friends and relatives. Tasty food, complementary wines, fine friends, insightful conversation. What could be better?

Well, knowledgeable service, quality glassware and fair prices, for a start. Sadly, the restaurant wine experience frequently fails to live up to the ideal. Occasionally it's that old voodoo of the snooty sommeliers who think they alone hold the key to the mysteries of wine. More often it's plain old ignorance-cum-lack-of-enterprise that scuttles your celebratory plans.

One warning sign: No wine glasses on the table. Only the absence of forks would be worse, I suppose. Warning sign two: Wines priced twice or thrice *retail*. Aieee. There's no good reason for any bottle of wine to cost more than twice the wholesale cost, and when an average wine costs more than the entrées…I walk.

Restaurants that handle wine best have waiters who know their wine lists intimately, which means nothing short of having tasted most or all of the wines offered. I know chefs who routinely have their staff taste wines with entrées so that they know which matches work best and can recommend them with confidence.

Despite my own extensive experience, I delight in asking wine waiters (and retail clerks) for their recommendations. That's how, some years ago, I first discovered the delights of Cahors, a then unknown French red made from Malbec. It was a wine I would not otherwise have ordered—save for the waiter's informed suggestion—and it made our meal all the more memorable of an experience.

Restaurant wine lists range from disappointing to intimidating. I've run into everything from the jokester's classic—"1. Red, 2. White, 3. Rosé. Please order by number."—to unwieldy lists that seem to include nearly every wine from every region on the planet. Who needs that?

One of my fantasies is to have a restaurant hire me to write a tightly drawn, concise list of, say, two dozen wines. I would pick wines representative of a variety of styles, complete with brief descriptions of each wine and what menu items each might best complement or contrast them. That way, patrons wouldn't have to spend more time with the wine list than with the menu, and they'd be able to get on to the more satisfying business of conversation, food, and wine.

Increasing numbers of restaurant owners are getting it these days, offering to pour you wine by the bottle, by the glass, or even by the "taste" (two ounces, usually). That way, you can "graze" your way through the wine list much in the manner that you might order several appetizers and "graze" your way through the menu. It's a great way to test wine and food combinations that you might otherwise never consider. (It is especially thoughtful to offer dessert wines by-the-glass. Makes a favorable, lasting last impression.)

One last word on wine in the restaurant. For more than a decade—in California, Oregon, and some other states—it has been legal for a diner to take home any wine not consumed in the restaurant. Some staffs are not aware of this, but it's the law and it's a good one. No point in trying to finish up a bottle...only to end up a touch past your driving ability, just to ensure that you get what you paid for. Just cork up the bottle, put it in your trunk, and have it for lunch the next day with the contents of your doggie bag.

conclusion

The "Philosophy" of Wine

Philosophy is the means by which we examine things, shine a light upon them to discover what true meaning exists.

In college, my first roommate was a Peruvian fellow whose immediate antecedents were mixed, to say the least. His mother was Peruvian and Catholic, his father a Russian Jew. Jorge referred to himself as "multifacetic," meaning that he had many facets.

That, in a created word, is the strength of the wine business. Wine is something of a cultural hub. It is "multifacetic," in that it draws upon such a wide variety of facets for its melded strength. Wine is first, of course, telluric, being of the *soil*, drawing from the art and incantation that is agriculture. But it is also science, taking much from university learning; it is technology, from stainless steel to iron-boned harvesters; it is art, whereby the craftsman culls layered nuance from mere grape juice.

But wine also draws from literature, religion, and the related business skills that encompass everything from marketing and advertising to sales and accounting. Where many conversations hit shallow waters soon after the speaker's area of expertise is exhausted, wine folk only begin to get interesting when they are lured away from the *vino*. Wine, in short, is an encompassingly cosmopolitan business, one of great depth and breadth. "Multifacetic" fits.

Piero Antinori is a man who understands the depth of the business, his family having tilled Italian vinelands for more than six centuries. (Say that aloud. Six centuries. Beyond the obvious alliteration, it kind of takes your breath away, doesn't it?) This is a man who sees the philosophical grounding of wine as well as any.

"Wine has been, since the dawn of days, a product made to give pleasure," says Antinori by way of preface. "If we think about the ancient Greeks and Romans, they used to call it nectar or ambrosia, and it was considered the real luxury; there was also a wine god, Bacchus, to confirm this. Wine was shipped all over the Mediterranean as a very precious item.

"Centuries went by and we always find notes talking about the pleasure to which wine drinking was tied to, from Popes to Kings, all over Europe. A quality wine can contribute to the understanding—together with food—of a land, of its culture, tradition, and of its people. A wine is produced by the winemaker after he has profoundly understood the soil and the climate where his vines are grown, after he has understood the traditional winemaking of the area and re-elaborated that in a modern style. This is an important point, as 'modern' can not mean just 'different' but it has to contain the focal points of the precedent tradition. Tradition means art, science, poetry, and economics of the area.

"When you drink a good bottle of wine, you should think of the kind of work there is behind it, not only technical but philosophical. The wine itself should be able to transmit, together with food, a small part of the taste of where it was born, of the character, and history of the people that have grown it."

One of my favorite vinous philosophers is Bonny Doon's Randall Grahm, who is always capable of seeing an issue from some slanted angle that intrigues. "What wine really is about is transport or transformation—not merely or chiefly the fact that we may become slightly or more than slightly intoxicated. With any luck, a fine bottle will give us a new and different perspective on things. Wine is a magical kaleidoscopic instrument that can change everything. We might imagine the experience of a wine as the mere sum of its component parts—grapes and wood and dirt—but, in fact, wine represents the complete transformation of these mute elements. Dusky, ripe clusters of grapes are somehow metamorphosed into a potpourri of complex and exotic flavors—cedar, black currant, sandalwood, and a handful of other spices and fragrances that we can't quite identify. Suddenly wine will put us in touch with a hidden emotion or an unbidden memory. In its finest moments a wine will move us to poetry or to song."

Grahm is convinced that we human folk have to look behind facades to get to the important truths. "We do not particularly learn our lessons when they are out in front of us, or presented to us in ordinary language. Our deepest lessons are learned when we experience them viscerally, that is to say metaphorically, and wine is, in essence, pure metaphor. It shows us the way that an element from one order of existence can become another, and dares us to make great leaps of imagination. It is itself the product of infinitely complex transformation; mutability is its *carte de visite* [calling card]. So wine's greatest and secret lesson is that everything is capable of change, including us. Maybe this is why wine will comfort us in ways that we barely apprehend—for me, its wisest gift."

In the end, it is that direct connection with the earth that offers the best philosophical lessons. For farmers are folk who most truly understand the Zen incantation "go with the flow." For these are citizens who—when faced with flood and failure—simply shrug their shoulders and mutter quietly, "Hey, we'll get 'em next year!" Not a bad philosophy.

Expand Your Palate's Horizons:
One New Wine Each Month

I collect quotations, and one of my favorites involves expanding the way you look at life by opening your mind and your "selves" to new experience. It was the great Supreme Court jurist, Oliver Wendell Holmes Jr. who advised, "A mind expanded by a new idea never returns to its former size."

Thus I suggest to you, try a new wine at least once a month. As you might imagine, there will be many that you will find ordinary, even mundane. But every once in awhile, you'll pick a wine that will blaze across your palate like a shooting star across the firmament, and that will prove the exercise's value once and for all. I remember the first time I tasted Andrew Quady's "Electra," a low alcohol (four percent) Muscat. Wow! It was delicate, fresh, and zingy with that floral-grape essence of Muscat, all in a wine that I could sip all afternoon to my contentment. What a find!

Open your palate to delectable new tastes from dazzling new places. We've all seen and tasted the excitement of New Zealand Sauvignon Blancs over the last decade or so, and the wines coming out of South Africa today are worthy of your considered attention. Who knows where the next thrilling "place" will be. Rumania? Georgia (in the former Soviet Union)? Georgia (in the good old US of A)? The world is your vinous oyster, and if you're not trying new things, you are apt to miss out, big time. Create the expectation, the self-fulfilling prophecy you desire, then fulfill it. Be willing to be amazed . . . and you surely will be.

And Don't Forget...

- **Can't finish a bottle?** There are fancy vacuum and CO_2 thingees available to prevent oxidation in an unfinished bottle. Here are two low-tech solutions, absent expensive gadgets that often work poorly anyway: Just decant what you're not going to drink into a half bottle [375 ml]; or drop marbles into the bottle to raise the liquid level back to the top. Either way works just fine until you get around to the finishing the bottle.

- **Need to decant a wine?** Modern day wines are made clean—fined and filtered to a perfect clarity—so there's rarely a need to decant a wine. When you do come across a wine that's a bit cloudy in bottle, or you just want to expose the wine to oxygen to allow it to open up a bit—useful with young, super-sized reds—decanting is a good idea. You want to pour the wine into another vessel or decanter, using a light source behind the neck of the bottle as you pour (we used to use candles, now a flashlight works just fine) so that you can cease pouring when you get to the cloudy part.

- **How long should wine be aged in bottle?** There's no hard and fast rule, unfortunately. Some wines are best right away—this is true of reds and whites alike—and others are best after a decade or more softening, maturing, gaining complexity in bottle. Part of the equation depends on how we were weaned on wine: Europeans tend to like older, oxidized, more complex wines; Americans and Aussies have a fondness for fresh fruit, the younger the better. Great White Rieslings get oily and viscous after a decade or so, while Beaujolais is best right off the store's shelf. As always, the more you taste, the more certain you'll be as to what best suits your own inclinations.

The Bottom Line

The whole and entire purpose of this slender volume is to nudge you to the point of trusting, even glorifying your own palate. It's like the old African proverb (you ever met a young proverb?) says, "Until lions have their historians, all tales of hunting will glorify the hunter."

To date, virtually all of the wine books ever written have glorified wine. Which is fine, up to a point. And that point comes when you, the consumer, decide to claim your own palate by renouncing the judgments from on high by wine critics. All wine critics, humble and proud alike. Your palate is yours, and yours alone. No one—not me, not Robert Parker Jr., not Jim Laube, not anyone—can talk precisely to your palate. You are the only person on this whirling orb who knows what you love, what you'll tolerate, and what absolutely turns your tongue to dirt.

In the three-plus decades that I've worked in wine, it has continually puzzled me that the same person who would never let someone else dictate his or her taste in any of the arts...turns around and asks "What wine should I like?" After all that time, I've finally come up with a quick retort—this book is the long retort—"Taste 10 wines, you'll like three, you can afford two...those are the two to buy!"

What we're after here, is two-fold: We want to find wines that give us pleasure and we want to find wines that we can afford to buy on a regular basis. For one person that might mean Fetzer and Kendall-Jackson, for another it might mean Chateau Latour and Screaming Eagle. So long as you know the difference. That's the bottom line.

Index

Credits

Good Wine: the new basics Copyright © 2005 by Silverback Books, Inc.
Text © 2005 Richard Paul Hinkle

Production Team

Project editor: Lisa M. Tooker
Editor: Pamela D'Angelo
Layout and production: Patty Holden

Food stylist: Pouké for front cover, 12, 23, 27, 31, 52, 55, 158
Prop stylist: Carol Hacker/Tableprops for front cover, 12, 23, 27, 31, 52, 55, 130–131, 158
Props courtesy of Sur La Table: 12, 23, 27, 31, 52, 55, 130–131, 158
Wine bottles provided by Paul Marcus Wines: 12, 23, 27, 31, 130–131, 158
Wine glasses provided by Bottego del Vino: 67

ISBN 1-930603-78-9

Printed in China

Photo Credits

Front Cover: Lisa Keenan
Barrow/StockFood: 82; Benelux Press/StockFood: 120, 123, 132, 142; Boch/StockFood: 38, 99; Bottego del Vino: 67; Campbell/StockFood: 49, 88; Cardinale/StockFood: 62; Carrier/StockFood: 15, 24, 56; Cephas-Christodolo/StockFood: 112, 115; Cephas Picture Library/StockFood: 85, 96, 100, 103, 107, 108, 124, 126, 138; Cephas-Rock/StockFood: 95, 111, 116; Cephas-Stefanski/StockFood: 19; Eising FoodPhotography/StockFood: 2, 145, 152; Element Photo/StockFood: 16; Erricson/StockFood: 8; Goerlach/StockFood: 73; Gottlieb/StockFood: 80; Green/StockFood: 36; Richard Paul Hinkle: 74, 76, 119; Langlois/StockFood: 60–61; La Phototeque/StockFood: 84; Lisa Keenan Photography: 12, 23, 27, 31, 52, 55, 130–131, 158; Lehmann/StockFood: 20, 50, 59, 146; Maehl/StockFood: 137; Maxx Images-Sherlock/StockFood: 79; Montana/StockFood: 150; Neunsinger/StockFood: 70; Okolicsanyi/StockFood: 92; Sarpa/StockFood: 4, 42, 90; Schaffer/Smith/StockFood: 45, 89, 129; Schieren/StockFood: 11; Silver Visions Publishing Co., Inc./StockFood: 104; Skipper/StockFood: 28; Spathis & Miller/StockFood: 32; Wallach/StockFood: 68; Worrell/StockFood: 151

The Author

Richard Paul Hinkle is, by his very nature, singularly suited to write this "basic" wine book. Not only has he spent his career working to demystify wine—this is his eighth wine book—he also has an eclectic approach to life: It is not solely informed by wine.

"The best wines are creations of balance, from vineyard to fermentation," says Hinkle, the deucedly proud father of teen twins. "So, too, should a life have balance between our four 'selves': the physical self, the mental self, the social self, and the spiritual self. You need them all to create a vital, satisfying life." Hinkle lives an active and diverse life, having previously spent time as a deputy sheriff, a firefighter, and a professional baseball player ("all the things you dream of as a kid"). He continues to play hardball on a "50+" team, has built his own house, has flown a small plane across the country (twice), and is teaching himself to speak Spanish and to play Irish and Bluegrass fiddle.

"You have to have something out there on the horizon to keep you pointed in the right direction," he says with a laugh. "This wonderful project—the slender volume you are presently reading—is designed to help you understand that you can choose what you like when it comes to wine, and that wine can just as easily—maybe more easily—be enjoyed in the absence of the pomp and circumstance, without the tuxedo, the black tie, the formal dress, and all the pretension and arrogance that too often accompanies it. Just get some wine in a good glass, savor it slowly, and enjoy! It's not nearly as hard as it looks, as some would make it out to be. All of that nonsense should be their problem, not yours. So, just enjoy. Really, it's as easy as that."

Favorite Wines and Wineries

_____

_____

_____

_____

_____

_____

_____

_____

_____

_____

_____

_____

_____